Contents

The Principal Difference

Key issues in school leadership and how to deal with them successfully

SUSAN CHURCH

Pembroke Publishers Limited

To Barbara Comber, thesis supervisor without equal

© 2005 **Pembroke Publishers**
538 Hood Road
Markham, Ontario, Canada L3R 3K9
www.pembrokepublishers.com

Distributed in the U.S. by Stenhouse Publishers
480 Congress Street
Portland, ME 04101-3400
www.stenhouse.com

We acknowledge the financial support of the Government of Canada through the Book Publishing Industry Development Program (BPIDP) for our publishing activities.

We acknowledge the support of the Government of Ontario through the Ontario Media Development Corporation Book Fund.

Library and Archives Canada Cataloguing in Publication

Church, Susan M.
      The principal difference : key issues in school leadership and how to deal with them / Susan Church.

Includes index.
ISBN 1-55138-193-1

      1. School principals. 2. School management and organization.
I. Title.

LB2831.9.C48 2005   371.2'012   C2005-903728-8

Editor: Kat Mototsune
Cover Design: John Zehethofer
Typesetting: JayTee Graphics

Printed and bound in Canada
9 8 7 6 5 4 3 2 1

Introduction

"Why would anyone *want* to be a principal?" retorted many of the most gifted teachers I tried to recruit into educational administration when I was a school district administrator. Why *would* someone want to give up the rewards of working with young people to deal with piles of paperwork; with the often contradictory demands of teachers, parents, and the educational bureaucracy; with eighty-hour work weeks; and with an unending parade of school reform initiatives? What aspect of the job could possibly attract an intelligent, thoughtful, and student-focused educator to such a job? What could hold an experienced administrator, such as the talented principal I know who left her job to teach internationally several years before her planned retirement date? She told me, "My job had become so difficult and stressful that I couldn't wait for retirement to come." I believe that there is some urgency in answering these questions. We desperately need gifted educational leaders at a time when quality public education is more important than ever, as we prepare the children and youth of today — and tomorrow — to live and work in a rapidly changing and complex post-industrial world.

Learning from Research and Life Experiences

I don't claim to have all the answers for how public education can best attract and hold intelligent, creative, and skilled people as teachers and leaders. I do, however, have some insights gained through nearly three decades of experience in public education, as a teacher and administrator, and through doctoral work related to organizational change and leadership. Both my work and research have helped me understand what a complex and challenging role it is to lead in increasingly diverse educational contexts. It's not a job for someone who needs predictability, routine, and certainty. It's a job that demands much, but it can also return much. Even in today's context, in which principals find themselves increasingly bombarded by conflicting demands, I believe that it is still possible for school leaders to make positive differences for children and youth. Moreover, I do not believe that a woman or man has to be a superhero or to sacrifice health and relationships with family and friends to do so.

Part of what motivated me to do research was my desire to explore how leadership could be reconceptualized so that people other than self-sacrificing superheroes (or those motivated primarily by status or power) might feel more inclined to become, and to then remain, school administrators. I wanted to make sense of my own work as an assistant superintendent, to gain insights into the effects of educational reforms in school communities, and to imagine ways in which relationships across the levels of the organization could better support both student learning and professional growth. I also wanted to rethink theories and practices of leadership in light of both my own research and the professional and scholarly literature related to educational leadership and reform. As part of my investigation, I interviewed several district-level administrators, as well as the principal, vice-principal, teachers, parents, and students from one school community as the focus of a case study.

When I tackled the literature review as part of my research, I found the task more than a little daunting. I spent months sifting through hundreds of books, articles, and research studies. I was struck by how apt was the characterization of the collective inquiry into educational leadership as "many and disparate voices on the leadership stage" (Riley & Louis, p. 8). I wondered at the time how an educational leader, engaged full-time in a teaching or administrative job, could ever keep up, much less make sense of it all. Given the volume of material published — in print and electronic forms — it's not a mystery why practitioners often say, "I don't have time for a lot of theory; just give me practical suggestions for how I can do my job better."

Rethinking Leadership

Why should practitioners take the time to understand the conceptual and theoretical issues regarding the nature of leadership that are of such interest to researchers? What relevance do such issues have for those currently in leadership roles or for teachers considering a move into administration?

Based on my reading of the research, the shifts in thinking in leadership theory over the past decade or so hold hopeful possibilities. These theoretical frameworks could be the basis for the development of leadership practices that are both responsive to the complexities of today's educational contexts and also sustainable over the long term.

Definitions of leadership are evolving from conceptions that identify and describe the characteristics and practices of *individuals* in administrative roles to descriptions of *relational processes* that constitute leadership. For example, researchers Riley and Louis (p. xv) conceptualize leadership

> …not as a role-based function assigned to, or acquired by, a person in an organisation, who uses his or her power to influence the actions of others, but as a network of relationships among people, structures and cultures (both within and across organisational boundaries).

Enacting Relational Leadership

Leithwood and Duke conclude an extensive review of a century of school leadership research with the call for a research agenda aimed at "developing a more comprehensive account of leadership based upon relationships" (p. 65). They identify four sets of interacting elements — the leader, the follower, the organization, and the environment — and argue that "the most complex and important aspects of leadership are to be found in the nature of the relationships themselves. How can such relationships adequately be conceptualized?" (p. 67).

As my doctoral research evolved, I became intrigued by the problem inherent in that question and attempted to make some contribution to answering it. The question is of theoretical importance, but it also has implications for leadership practices at all levels of education. The notion of leadership as something other than a role-based function is hard to pin down because it is complex, dynamic, multifaceted, and non-linear. The challenge of theorizing about "networks of relationships" is difficult enough. Thinking through how administrators and teachers might do their jobs, how organizations might structure themselves, and how interactions across levels of the organization and beyond might play out in response to such a relational theory of leadership is a substantive project. That project will certainly be advanced through research, but it also depends upon the beliefs and actions of individuals in the contexts in which they are working.

Many conceptions of teaching and leadership attempt to simplify these complexities through lists: the fifteen characteristics of effective schools, or the five most significant lessons of reform, or the ten most important features of successful principals. These simplistic conceptions contrast with relational theories of leadership. Almost twenty years ago, Roland Barth critiqued the "list logic" that seems to pervade educational change initiatives. Barth argued that "Lists tend to be prescriptions for other people and for other people's children. Most external lists constitute a suffocating description of a teacher's job, a principal's job, or a pupil's job." He went on to observe that, "I doubt that we would find many teachers, principals, and students in high achieving schools comply closely with a list of any kind." (p. 294). I trust readers will interpret the lists in this book as they are intended — they do not represent my "expert's" formula on how to be a principal; rather, they provide possibilities for practice to consider.

Exploring Issues in School Leadership

I believe that schools and school systems can change, both to enhance our success in meeting the needs of the increasingly diverse students in our care and to create workplaces in which adults find meaning and purpose in their work.

I came to the end of my doctoral studies with a broader and deeper conceptualization of the issues I had investigated, but also with many new questions I have continued to explore. Having moved on from leadership in public education to my current work as a teacher-educator, researcher, and consultant, I am still actively engaged in grappling with the complexities of school leadership, both theoretically and practically. I observe many friends and colleagues still working as school and school-district administrators who are struggling to cope with increasingly demanding accountability systems, with roles that are more managerial than educative, and with competing expectations from diverse publics.

This book is for them and others like them. It offers a perspective on several current issues in education, considering not only how they influence school leadership but also how practices of relational leadership might enhance administrators' capacities to respond to these issues. Chapter 1 focuses on how principals can create and sustain professional learning communities by working collaboratively with their staff members. In Chapter 2, the focus shifts beyond those who work in the school to explore ways of engaging students, parents, and other community members as active partners in learning. The chapter also discusses relationships between schools and the larger educational organizations of which they are a part. Chapter 3 addresses how principals can respond proactively to the increasing racial and cultural diversity in their schools. In Chapter 4, I explore the implications of recent research on gender and schooling, providing suggestions for ways schools can support the learning of both boys and girls. Chapter 5 tackles the challenge schools face in responding to expectations for accountability. In Chapter 6, I examine the tension between management and leading in the work of principals, and provide a perspective on how school leaders can successfully do both. I conclude with some thoughts on why I think the job of principal is worth doing. Readers who wish to explore the issues further will find all the resources cited in the text listed in the bibliography. As well, a number of helpful web sites are included in margin notes.

Each of the issues discussed in this book — creating professional learning communities, inviting parents to be active participants and supporters of their children's learning, responding to multicultural and gender diversity, orchestrating leading and managing, and taking responsibility for improving student achievement — relates to all the others. In the work lives of principals, these issues and others are in constant interplay. For example, as soon as a principal begins to work towards the creation of a learning community in a school, he or she must grapple with issues of diversity. Processes and structures must enhance the collaborative community without silencing diverse perspectives.

Woven throughout the book are the words of participants in my doctoral research. Their voices animated my dissertation and will, I hope, resonate with readers of this book. I am indebted to them all for their generosity and honesty in sharing their perspectives on leadership, schooling, and change. There is particular emphasis on how Laura (a pseudonym), the principal of the school, viewed her work. Her reflections give a human face to the complex job of leading a school.

I constructed the following poetic transcript from several conversations that I had with Laura over one school year. For me, the poem powerfully evokes the tensions associated with school leadership. It shows the vulnerabilities, uncertainties, and emotional upheaval associated with the principal's work, but Laura's concluding comments provide a hopeful commentary on the positive possibilities that are emerging from her struggles and those of the teachers.

IT'S A STRUGGLE

It's hard, hard work.
It's difficult.
I was afraid
That was what they were looking for
I knew
I wasn't going to deliver.

I struggle with that…
It's just like pulling teeth
It is going to be a struggle.
I struggled with that,
With the teacher.
They struggle.

But it's a struggle and it's very complex.
Whatever the struggle may be
That's a struggle for me.

They're struggling,
Oh wow, are they struggling with that program.
I'm struggling with it already;
I don't even want to talk about it.
I feel tremendously guilty.

They struggle with that
It's rushed and I struggle.
I struggle with that, too.
So, it's a struggle for some people.

We always seem to be putting out fires
And putting band-aids on this.
We never seem to get to the root
Of what it is
That makes our school so busy.

My focus has been
On building relationships
With everybody
Who works in that building.
Start with the trust,
First.
And build that rapport.
That was my focus
Before anything else.

Things have started to change a little bit.
Things seem to be a little less turbulent
And a little less chaotic.
Today was a bit wingy
But generally there's been a change.
I feel it.
I feel it in the office.
And I feel it with the kids.
And I feel it in the staff room.

When I got there
I felt it was a very tense place to work.
And I don't any more.

CHAPTER 1   Professional Learning Communities

Many schools are coping with extensive staff turnover, as large numbers of teachers leave the profession through retirement and new teachers take their places.

In the field of educational leadership, there is currently broad consensus regarding the power of collaborative professional learning communities to positively affect student learning. If creating collaborative relationships were simply a matter of following a sequence of steps or a list of to-dos, every school would be a professional learning community. I question the helpfulness of the advice circulating in current educational journals and books, because too often it ignores the uncertain and changing contexts in which today's leaders are working.

Therefore, it seems to me that school leaders need to begin with the assumption that they will be working towards collaborative practices in dynamic, constantly changing school contexts. They will not be able to count on long-term consistency in staff. People will come and go from the learning community. Schools are continuously in response mode as they deal with externally mandated reform initiatives; changes in government often bring entirely new agendas, sometimes contradictory to what went before. Vital and sustainable professional learning communities thus need to be constructed as living, changing entities, able to respond to unexpected internal and external events through rethinking and sometimes regrouping. The consistency in purpose and direction comes through the leader's words and actions and through processes and structures that support collaborative work practices that have a focus on student learning.

The Nature of Professional Learning Communities

Current conceptions of professional learning communities coalesce around several central features:

- a focus on ensuring that all students learn
- teachers working together to improve their practices
- ongoing use of many sources of information to monitor student achievement

Schools that are professional learning communities look very different from the places that most of us have experienced as students and as teachers. In such communities, emphasis shifts from teaching (What activities are occurring in the classroom?) to learning (How and to what extent are the classroom experiences promoting learning for all students?). Teachers make public their traditionally private, closed-door practices through ongoing interactions around student learning and their own work. Everyone in the school takes responsibility for monitoring student achievement, and all are accountable for outcomes.

These are huge shifts for most teachers and administrators. This is messy and difficult work. In studies of teachers' work cultures, Canadian researcher Andy

Collaborative contexts are spontaneous, voluntary, development-oriented, pervasive across time and space, and unpredictable; contrived collegiality is administratively regulated, compulsory, implementation-oriented, fixed in time and space, and predictable.

Hargreaves (1994) documents how administrators attempting to promote collaboration and collegiality often coerce teachers into working together by mandating practices such as team teaching, even when there are substantive differences in beliefs among the teachers involved. Who protects the rights of individuals to work alone or to disagree with each other in these situations? In other settings, administrators use collaborative practices to co-opt teachers into adopting mandated curricular changes, using group processes to force consensus and commitment rather than to invite participation and critique. Administrators driven by the need to control often stifle initiatives in which teachers or staff and community members would spontaneously collaborate because of shared interests and goals, substituting what Hargreaves calls "contrived collegiality."

The Importance of Trust

School-improvement research over several decades shows that the nature and quality of social relationships in school communities are key factors in either enhancing or impeding efforts to improve student learning. For example, drawing on evidence from longitudinal research into school reform in Chicago, Bryk and Schneider identify the development of trust as a central feature of the relationships that characterize the more successful schools. The researchers describe how the principal of one of the highest-achieving schools interacted extensively with staff, emphasizing the moral responsibility of the school to advance the education and welfare of the students in their care. Statistical evidence supports the positive impact of the relational trust built through these leadership practices on student achievement. The researchers identify four specific aspects of this process:

- In a context in which there is relational trust, teachers feel less vulnerable to try new practices and to make changes.
- In such a context there are greater possibilities for collective teacher work and group problem solving.
- Relational trust supports the development of group norms that create pressure and incentive for all teachers to engage in continual learning and enhancement of classroom practices. Without relational trust, teachers are more likely to remain in their classrooms, struggling on their own.
- With trusting relationships come stronger personal attachments and greater commitment to the purposes of the school, along with a willingness to expend greater efforts to accomplish group goals.

Bryk and Schneider conclude that "trust fosters a set of organizational conditions, some structural and others social-psychological, that make it more conducive for individuals to initiate and sustain the kinds of activities necessary to affect productivity improvements" (p. 116).

The researchers also document the challenges and complexities of building and sustaining such relationships. Further emphasizing this point, Schmoker examines the evidence in support of the development of professional learning communities and expresses his frustration that "such collaboration — our most effective tool for improving instruction — remains exceedingly, dismayingly rare" (p. 431).

Although such collaboration may be rare, it does exist. While there is no recipe for school leaders to follow in creating collaborative professional learning communities in the diverse contexts in which they work, individuals can learn from the knowledge base that has evolved over the past decade. So, how do leaders move forward in creating professional learning communities, while avoiding the pitfalls Hargreaves and others have described?

Setting an Example

Leaders have to begin with their own words and actions. These provide the most powerful means through which they can establish expectations for others and demonstrate what it means to live and work collaboratively.

As I observed Laura over the several months that I shadowed her in the school, I noted the impact she had through the accumulation of numerous small interactions with staff members. In my interviews with eleven of the teachers a consistent message came through. They all identified the leader's ability to create and sustain collaborative and supportive working relationships as the primary quality they valued in this school's administrative team (the principal and vice-principal) and others with whom they had worked in the past. The teachers identified a number of specific features of the leader's behavior that contributed to these positive relationships:

- listening
- responding to questions and concerns
- being accessible (the office door is always open)
- providing help when needed rather than blaming
- showing appreciation, giving recognition, validating others
- demonstrating respect for and acceptance of diverse perspectives
- celebrating creativity
- offering constructive criticism
- providing materials
- offering professional reading and professional development opportunities

One teacher told me,

> For me, what's important in administration is their support. I feel like I'm appreciated for what I do. And I'm supported in any ideas I have. And it's positive. I don't mind criticism as long as it is constructive. And to feel part of a team, that the team is supporting me and you get to see them as a person and they respect you as a person.

The teacher describes a leader who puts people first. She defines "support" in terms of the one-to-one relationship the principal has with her: the appreciation shown; the acceptance of ideas; and the feedback, both positive and constructively critical. The leader also fosters relationships among the staff in which the same one-to-one connection is important: "you get to see them as a person and they respect you as a person." Unlike the examples of contrived collegiality, this school leader is shown to work at opening dialogue and inviting diverse perspectives. She and other leaders like her understand that relationships are made or broken through their daily interactions with staff.

From the beginning of her tenure as principal Laura consciously led by example rather than exhortation:

> I had to sort of jump in and go, and I can only be who I am, so when I spoke to them the first day of school, I said that I suspected that many of them were expecting me to tell them what kind of leader I am and to give sort of a brief explanation of what I

expected of them. And I proceeded to tell them that my leadership does not come in a can or a package and you don't add water and there it is — presto. If they want to know what kind of a leader I am, then they should watch me. And that's all I told them: just watch me and it won't take you long to figure out where my head is.

The Central Place of Conversation

When I first moved from a school into a district leadership role, I remember vividly words of advice from a more experienced administrator: that I would need to close my office door in order to get any work done. If not, I would be constantly interrupted by people coming in to talk to me. As I thought about that, I realized that she and I had a totally different notion about what our work was. While she was concerned about getting her reports written and her e-mail read, I concluded that my most important work was ongoing interaction with staff — interruptions reconstituted as purposeful dialogue. It was through those conversations, not through directives or policies, that I had the biggest impact on what happened in the schools in the area of the district for which I was responsible.

Some of the conversation was the kind of social talk that characterizes positive relations in any setting: sharing delight or dismay about the weather (a preoccupation of those who live in cold climates such as Canada's), talking about activities outside school, asking about family members, or noting others' accomplishments. Most of the interactions, however, moved beyond the strictly social to focus on the work of the schools and the district — enhancing the learning of all students in whatever ways we could. I demonstrated my confidence in staff by treating them as professionals; I expected them to be able to articulate the rationale for their decisions as well as to contribute their expertise and informed perspectives to the issues that confronted me as the leader. As a leader, I demonstrated what I valued and expected of staff through my informal interactions. I asked questions about how decisions would affect learners: How does this help students? What is the thinking behind this decision or practice? How can I support you? I also made visible the thinking behind my own decisions, saying such things as, "This is how I am thinking of handling this issue in the best interests of the students, what do you think?" Or, "Can you see any pitfalls in what I am planning to do?" In turn, staff would come to me to get feedback on decisions they were making or problems that they had to solve.

> Laura had many face-to-face interactions with staff. Here is how she described her efforts to reach out:
>
> > When I go to work I try to get out of the office. I try to get down to the staff room, I try to connect with teachers, I try to listen to them. I want to know what is important to them and, if it's a need, then how can we work as a team to address it? If I discover a strength, then how can I foster that strength? And maybe there's some leadership in the staff and how can we make it grow?
>
> She regularly posed questions or wrote comments on the white board in the staff room, and invited teachers to respond to her in writing. The staff also used this space to acknowledge staff accomplishments and to celebrate important individual and collective events, from birthdays to special student activities. These ongoing written conversations helped to sustain

Throughout the twenty years that I worked in different district leadership roles, I not only kept the office door open, but I also walked out of the office as often as I could to keep the conversations going.

communications when everyone was too busy to have time for face-to-face conversations everyday. Laura also posted the draft staff-meeting agendas and asked all staff members — teachers and support staff — to add items they wished to have discussed. This alerted her to what was on the minds of staff and to issues — often contentious — that might be brewing. As a result, she was better able to facilitate productive problem solving before and during staff meetings.

Living with Differences

The white board is one practical way this principal enhanced the capacity of her learning community to live and work together harmoniously and productively, while still expressing their individuality. She made it safe for people to express their opinions and to voice different perspectives. Although she made clear her own vision for the school, emphasizing her commitment to student learning above all, she created space for teachers to exercise professional judgement. One of the teachers commented,

> I feel I am quite free to teach in a style that I'm comfortable with. I don't feel that anyone's breathing down my neck to be sure that I'm toeing the line when it comes to curriculum, although I tend to do that anyway. I feel there is quite a bit of professional freedom.

Yet, it was clear that the school administrators walked a fine line between validating each teacher's philosophy and setting pedagogical expectations. As one teacher put it, "They validate the instruction that I am giving to the students — not all the instruction, but they validate my own philosophy, my thinking." When the teacher says "not all the instruction," she shows her awareness of the principal's bottom line — the students. Even in a professional learning community built on trusting relationships, there is sometimes tension between support for teachers and responsibilities to students. Not everyone sees the world the same way, but there are limits to the freedom of expression of personal philosophies when the well-being of students or of the school community as a whole is concerned.

I found it was helpful to keep Margaret Meek Spencer's wonderful question (in Dillon) in mind: What if it's otherwise? It gave me a place to begin when challenging a staff member to reconsider what they were doing or what they believed. The question opened dialogue and often led to generative new ways of thinking for both of us.

Laura stated the dilemma as follows:

> If what they are doing is not good for kids, then…it becomes difficult, more difficult to support them. I haven't been in a situation where there's been harm done to children, but I've had situations brought to my attention that something happened with a child and teacher that really was not nice and it needed to be addressed. And so, I guess I do it in a humane way and draw on whatever skills I have in dealing with people.

Determining when to encourage and support differing perspectives and when to challenge those that run counter to the best interests of the students or the school community is part of the art of leadership. Each person has to find his or her own bottom line in regard to what is negotiable. I always tried to remain open to the possibility that I had misinterpreted or did not fully understand the other person's perspective when I disagreed with a staff member's decision or a practice.

Leader as Head Learner and Head Teacher

Asking, "What if it's otherwise?" is a way of ensuring that everyone remains open to learning. I believe that it is particularly important for leaders to demonstrate that they are learners. If we expect staff members to learn and grow, we need to be the "head learners" in the group. Principals show they are learners when they

- buy and display professional resources in their offices and the school
- read articles and pass them along to individuals or groups of staff members with comments
- pass along interesting and relevant web sites or other electronic resources
- engage in professional development and talk about what they have learned with staff
- talk publicly about how they have changed their thinking or practices as a result of new learning
- see making time for professional conversations as a priority
- work in classrooms, demonstrating willingness to try out new practices alongside teachers, learning with them
- are not afraid to say, "I don't know."

Laura demonstrated her learning stance frequently, sometimes to the surprise of staff members like Mark (a pseudonym), her vice-principal. She recalled,

> He said to me he would never, ever have thought for one minute that, in a meeting with parents or staff or other teachers, when a question was asked, the principal would say, "Well, I don't know." And he said that he would have come from the thinking that when you become the principal of the school, you do know. So I thought that was very interesting. And I thought…well, I actually said to him, "God help me if I know everything!" Well, we laughed about it. And I said, there's no way that anybody can know everything. And, of course, it's okay to say, "I don't know."

Laura saw herself as the head teacher, the one responsible for helping teachers to grow in their theories and practices. When she came to the school, student discipline was a huge issue. Instead of imposing more rules, as some of the parents and teachers had demanded, she took a teaching/learning approach to the issue. Her focus included creating a more meaningful curriculum; providing more enjoyable activities for students before and after school, and during recess when many of the discipline issues arose; and teaching the students self-discipline. In her first few days in the school she became aware from observing the teachers that "these people are afraid of the principal and they're making their kids afraid of them."

Laura reflected on her first couple of years in the school as she worked with the teachers:

> I've tried to support them in that if they have difficulty with that shift in thinking, that's okay. That's learning and that's part of it and that it is going to be a struggle and, basically, are you in or not. Because that's where I'm going and I, to my knowledge, am not leaving for the next little while. And so if that is where my head is, that is where I would like to see the school go, I think it is my responsibility to lead the school. If I have people who support that philosophy of thinking and those who are struggling with it, we'll help you, we'll help you along.

Laura's efforts to change the ways in which adults interacted with students met with resistance from some of the teachers. She determined that the staff needed to get away from the school in order to work through the issues. She found funding to pay for an overnight staff retreat at a hotel, during which they spent time in small group discussions: some were formal, but many were over meals and "developing our collective vision through laughing together in the swimming pool and hot tub." She marked this retreat as a significant event in her tenure as principal. She talked about how she both learned and taught during the day-and-a-half they spent together, listening to the teachers' anger and fears and helping them to develop collective solutions to the problems that they raised. She described some of the discussions as being "hot and heavy" but absolutely necessary to moving forward as a staff.

Mutual Capacity Building

The school community's collective capacity to meet students' learning needs is built through reciprocal relationships among all members of the learning community.

When leaders position themselves both as learners and teachers, they reframe the concept of capacity building, one of the key roles identified for leaders in professional learning communities. Usually capacity building is defined in terms of the leader helping staff develop the skills and ability to share leadership responsibilities, to construct curriculum, and to contribute their expertise to the benefit of the school community. This implies a top-down process through which the leader, the holder of knowledge and skills, passes that knowledge along to staff members who lack the necessary insights and experiences to be fully participating co-leaders and decision makers. In contrast, mutual capacity building implies that the staff members have insights and knowledge that can support the leader's learning and growth. If leaders are open to learning from the other members of the school community, including parents and students (see Chapter 2), their capacities to lead will be enhanced.

Creating Supportive Structures and Processes

Administrators have the greatest ability and responsibility to configure the resources of the school in ways that enhance collaborative learning.

To state the obvious, every school is different. Therefore, the structures and processes that will be effective in one context may not be as helpful in another. The following describes practices that principals in a variety of contexts have adapted in response to the specific needs of their schools.

Making Time

For most teachers the biggest barrier to ongoing learning is lack of time. When I asked teachers in the case-study school what form of support would be most helpful to them, almost all of them answered, "More time!" Making time during the school day for professional development is a challenge. As demands on teachers and administrators have become more and more intense with the increased focus on results and accountability, instructional time has become more of an issue with systems and with the public. In highly centralized systems principals do not have much latitude to adjust instructional time and schedules to accommodate teacher professional development during the regular teaching day. In jurisdictions where such flexibility is still possible, either through district policies or school-level autonomy, such structural changes are significant supports for teacher growth.

Both the teachers and Laura mentioned how much they had appreciated a monthly early dismissal that provided an afternoon during which the staff could focus on professional development. The staff had used this time to meet in small groups to discuss curriculum initiatives, to share teaching practices, and to work on aspects of the school improvement plan. Unfortunately, lobbying by parents in another school in the district led to a district-wide policy that prohibited schools from banking time by lengthening the school day in order to dismiss students at noon one afternoon a month. Almost every staff member in the school mentioned the loss of the early dismissals as having a negative impact on their ability to engage in professional development.

The research on school improvement shows that an investment in teacher learning has a powerful positive impact on student achievement.

It is possible to find times during the school day when teachers can meet informally. This requires commitment on the part of staff and, as Laura explained with regret, can be difficult to sustain.

> Last year we ran monthly sessions at lunchtime called Math Chat. And a couple of teachers on staff would put on sessions for teachers and they would take a concept like data and probability, and they would develop all kinds of little games that you could play, dice games or card games or whatever that you could play with kids, that would get at the teaching of probability. And teachers came. They loved it. It was fun. They played games over the noon hour. And the person who did it doesn't have time this year. She said, "I just can't do it." So Math Chat went on for a year. And it was good while it lasted and I think teachers were feeling supported: "Okay, I can get through this." It also gave teachers an opportunity to talk: "Oh, I did that, I did that section in the book and it's the most disastrous. And so the next day I tried it this way." So there was some sharing going on with the math. That was last year. This year, there's been no talk of math at all.

Although there are limitations to what an individual principal can do to free up staff time for professional development, the following are some examples of what some principals have tried with success:

- Principals have taken over teachers' classrooms to free them to leave the school for professional development experiences, such as visits to other schools or attendance at workshops.

- Some schools have school funds that can be used to hire substitutes in order to release teachers.
- Administrators use staff-meeting time for professional development and find other means (handouts, e-mails) to communicate administrative information.

Job-embedded Staff Development

Traditional models of staff development create a separation between the work of teaching and the teacher as learner. Typically, teachers have four or five days a year set aside for professional development. The weaknesses of this model are well documented through the school improvement research. DuFour, one of the leading proponents of professional learning communities, writes, "School leaders must end this distinction between working and learning and create conditions that enable staff to grow and learn as part of their daily or weekly work routines" (p. 63). He goes on to identify four questions that need to guide job-embedded staff development:

The following approaches to job-embedded staff development have demonstrated positive results in a variety of schools:

- Reading/Study Groups
- Lesson Study
- Mentoring
- Action Research

- Does the professional development increase the staff's collective capacity to achieve the school's vision and goals?
- Does the school's approach to staff development challenge staff members to act in new ways?
- Does the school's approach to staff development focus on results rather than activities?
- Does the school's approach to staff development demonstrate a sustained commitment to achieving important goals?

I asked the teachers in Laura's school how they were best supported in implementing new curriculum mandated by the province. The first thing all of them mentioned was interaction with the staff and administrators in the school. One teacher said, "It's not even a matter of being in-serviced on the guides, but [the chance] to sit down and talk to other teachers that are at the same grade level and find out what they're doing." Another talked about the need for time for collective reflection. Laura commented on how little time was available for her teachers to engage in reflection:

> I think in our profession it's one of the areas that teachers have a thirst for and never get a chance to get at — just to sit and talk and reflect and talk. And, I mean, you can call it philosophy or whatever you want, but people, teachers, don't get a chance to talk about their practice.

Leaders must be intentional in their planning for staff interaction in order to address the questions that DuFour poses. There are a number of approaches that can be incorporated into the life of the school.

Reading/Study Groups One form of study group has a focus on the shared reading of professional articles and books. Teachers agree to meet regularly to discuss readings related to aspects of their practice. A leader can encourage this kind of activity by being an active participant, providing space and refreshments, and allocating funds to purchase reading materials.

Another focus of study groups can be the examination of student work. Teachers at a grade level might examine the writing their students are doing and discuss ways to support their further development. The entire staff might examine writing samples of students across grades to gain insights into the progress of students over time. A group of teachers might focus on what they can learn from one piece of writing or drawing, or other sample. The process of looking at student work involves

1. Choosing a small sample of work.
2. Examining that work with colleagues.
3. Reflecting on questions about teaching and learning.
4. Framing the observation and discussion through agreed upon guidelines (protocols). For example, teachers might agree upon the following steps: develop a focusing question; examine the work; share descriptions and observations; pose questions; give feedback to the presenting teacher; and then reflect on the process.

Lesson Study This is a professional development process that originated in Japan and is being incorporated in North American schools. It involves teachers systematically examining their practices by working together to plan and teach study lessons. In the Japanese context, this is the dominant form of professional development and usually has a focus on entire units of curriculum. The teachers agree upon an overarching goal and a related research question that they continually revisit as they work through the lessons they develop. The teachers develop the lesson plan together, one of the teachers teaches the lesson in a classroom as others observe, and then the group meets to discuss their observations. The discussions often lead to revisions of the lesson, and then the cycle is repeated. The final step is for the teachers to write a report on what they have learned.

Teachers need support in learning how to set appropriate goals, to craft research questions, to observe and to reflect on their observations. Principals can draw upon knowledgeable others to assist with this. Although lesson study is not widely practised in North America, most schools have access to district staff or university partners who have the expertise to help teachers develop the processes and skills needed. As teachers begin to develop experience and confidence with lesson study, the school can also draw upon expertise external to the school to expand teachers' content knowledge and to contribute energy and new ideas to the study groups.

Within North American schools the biggest challenge in incorporating lesson study is time. In Japan the school day is organized to include lesson study as an integral part of the teacher's work. Through creative use of existing resources, some principals have been able to schedule time during the school day, despite the limitations. A school in New Jersey pairs each classroom teacher with a non-classroom teacher (ESL, art, music, physical education, guidance, etc.). The partner teachers become familiar with classroom routines and student needs, and are scheduled in the classroom to free small groups of teachers for lesson study sessions. Other solutions to the time problem are implementing lesson study with a single grade level in a school, involving only a small group of teachers, or only partially implementing the process during a few weeks during the year.

Mentoring Informal mentoring relationships are common in schools in which there are caring and supportive relationships among staff. Often, more experienced teachers will "adopt" novice colleagues, helping them over the rough times

Further information on this professional development approach is available at www.lasw.org

Resources for developing lesson study are available online. Teachers College in New York City has a lesson research group that can be accessed at www.tc.edu/centers/lesson study. This site also provides links to other resources.

in the early stages of their careers. However, discouraging statistics continue to show large percentages of teachers leaving the profession in the first five years, and suggest that these informal alliances are not enough. Formalizing such relationships, like any other form of job-embedded professional development, requires additional resources or the creative use of existing resources. Time is an issue, as is the need for both mentors and mentees to understand how to work together productively.

A program at one urban school uses exemplary, recently retired teachers as mentors. These individuals are paid to work with less-experienced teachers two days a week, teaching model lessons as well as providing feedback on all aspects of curriculum and instruction. This program works well because the *mentor emeritus* does not have to worry about his or her own classroom responsibilities. As well, the program provides an opportunity for skilled professionals to remain purposefully engaged in the life and work of the school.

Action Research When teachers engage in action research, either individually or as a group, they design a process for inquiring critically into their own practices. Action research is a recursive process in which the interpretation of the data gathered leads to changes in practice and to the development of new questions to guide further research. It can be a powerful tool for engaging staff in continual reflection about their work.

The framework for such research is as follows:

1. Generate questions, concerns, or anomalies.
2. Generate data, for example,
   - observe and record (write, audio-tape, videotape, draw, photograph)
   - use journals or learning logs
   - collect documents and other artifacts
   - collect quantitative information
   - conduct structured or non-structured interviews
   - connect with professional literature
   - dialogue with colleagues
3. Analyze data
   - look for patterns and surprises
   - connect with professional literature
   - seek input from colleagues and others with expertise
4. Generate new questions.
5. Share the results with others.
6. Take action based on insights and generate new questions.

All these forms of job-embedded professional development — study groups of various sorts, mentoring, and action research — require a rethinking of teachers' work to include systematic inquiry into their own practices as an integral part of teaching. There is substantive research to show that investing in such professional development is key to improving student learning. Structures and expectations have to change, so that enhancing teachers' own learning becomes as big a priority for schools, school systems, and parents as maximizing teacher instructional time with students.

The mentoring example is described in the online newsletter of the Association for Supervision and Curriculum Development, *Classroom Leadership* (April 2005).

CHAPTER 2   Students, Parents, and the Wider Community

I heard time and again about Laura's open-door policy, fairness, willingness to listen, and human approach to interactions.

As I developed the school case study for my research, I was continually impressed with the myriad ways in which Laura reached out to build and sustain relationships with students, parents, and other community members. Their active involvement in the life of the school was evident, and both students and parents expressed their appreciation for that in their interviews.

Putting People First

Across all the interviews with parents and in a focus group with students, I heard time and again about Laura's open-door policy, fairness, willingness to listen, and human approach to interactions.

One parent told me,

> She's so fair. She's so open. Any parent can go to her at any time. Whether she agrees with you or not, she will find a way to solve your problem. She never makes a parent feel like they're stupid or you're overreacting. She's very fair. Her door is always open to any parent. I've never seen her turn anyone away. And the kids love her. She's very fair with the kids; she's firm but she's fair. She doesn't belittle kids. She doesn't yell at the kids; she makes them feel like they are actually human beings, which is something that a lot of them who were here during the previous principal were not used to.

This parent reiterates many of the points made by the teachers about the principal's openness and acceptance of different opinions. The speaker's use of "you" and "they" includes other parents; this is not her experience alone. Of most importance to this parent is the principal's respectful relationships with students. The negatives and the hint of sarcasm ("they are actually human beings") suggest that she has known very different sorts of school leaders, as she confirms in her last comment.

In the focus group with students, I began by asking what they would include if they were making a video about their school. Without prompting, they agreed that they would definitely want to show people how much they appreciated their principal. One student said, "Our principal is really good because she will listen to you no matter how weird [the issue is]. Like if you have a problem with a bus driver. If you tell her what happened, she'll call the bus company and tell them what happened and she'll listen to you." Another student gave a similar example, emphasizing the principal's persistence in following through on issues concerning students: "There was big problem with the lunch monitors but she's always on it. It's been going on for about two months. She really doesn't give up on anything." Further, the children emphasized the *way* in which the principal handled these situations, demonstrating her respect and the priority she places on relationships: "Whenever there's a problem, she doesn't just take you into the office and yap at you. She'll take you in and ask for both sides, even if it is a teacher [you are having a conflict with]. She just straightens it out without using her voice; she's really nice about it."

A parent offered another example of Laura's efforts on behalf of students, demonstrating how this leader took action based on her beliefs in respect and fairness.

> My son was ostracized in earlier grades and nothing was done about it. I talked a lot with the principal and it was really worked on. It wasn't let go and he's having a great year this year. And the other kids have heard so much about it. It's being nice to each other and kind to each other and I think it is finally hitting home. There's lots of opportunities to feel good about yourself here.

When the parent said, "It wasn't let go," it distinguished Laura from other leaders; the comparison was made ("Nothing was done about it"). Laura's impact was evident, not only on one student ("He's having a great year"), but also on the school as a whole ("It is finally hitting home").

As Laura neared the end of her third year in the school, she reflected on her philosophy,

> I guess my focus has been so much on building relationships with everybody who works in that building, whether it's students or teachers or support staff or parents in the community. That has been my focus every since I got there… [to] have that trust and… the kind of relationship with staff that we can have these conversations about language and scary language, like what are outcomes and what are Essential Graduation Learnings (EGLS). I can't start there; I have to start with the trust, first, and build that rapport. And that was my focus before anything else.

It was not totally smooth sailing when Laura came to the school. Parents had expectations that she would "clean up the discipline" through punitive measures. Instead, Laura engaged the students, staff, and parents in the process of becoming a peaceful school. Based on what I heard in the focus group with students, they understood that. They mentioned the assemblies in which peace was the focus and they proudly talked about receiving a flag from the Peaceful Schools organization: "It means that we've earned it, like we have learned peaceful ways. We have stuff in our classrooms; it's a cooperation kind of thing." They expressed pride in the student leadership program, through which children were taking responsibility among their peers for mediation and conflict resolution. The student leaders also organized activities on the playground to cut down on the fighting: "If someone is roughing it, then they would be banned because that's just not the way we should play." Laura's priority on shifting beliefs and practices about how people should treat each other was reflected in the children's responses.

In Laura's school, the focus was on developing respectful and trusting relationships.

Some parents, however, learned more slowly. Laura commented,

> There's a small, a very, very tiny part of the community who wishes that I would put the fear of god into kids. And when we talk about being a peaceful school, I get the impression that they, this small group of people, scoff at that because, on the heels of our peace conference, there were two kids in an altercation. And they're not understanding that it's a philosophy and that we're always, always working …we have to find better ways of dealing with conflict and go through the strategies yet again. For some kids it will take six years and for some it'll take six weeks and some don't need it. You know what I'm saying? And so, the parents who still subscribe to "the principal should rule with an iron fist," they're a small minority, but they exist, as well as the small minority of teachers that exist. But that's okay.

Laura restated her view that the changes she was working towards were at the philosophical level, and therefore "we're always, always working." There had been some *I told you so*s when two children got in a fight on the way home from school on the day the school held the peace conference. Laura understood that learning is ongoing and recursive, and that not all children learn on the same schedule or through similar experiences: "For some kids it will take six years and for some kids it's take six weeks and some don't need it." This was clearly an important point, so she checked that I understood: "You know what I'm saying?" Laura's conviction that she was going the right way, even though she was experiencing resistance from some teachers and parents, was captured in the last short sentence: "But that's okay." She seemed to be saying, "No one said this would be easy, but I'm up to it."

Whenever I was in the school, there seemed to be parents around in the hallways. Often, Laura was speaking with one or more of them as she went about her busy day.

"Recognize that most of the time you do not know what you are doing, and that you are probably, however unwittingly, often doing some harm or hurt to somebody. Be assured that there is always someone in the community who does not appreciate or benefit from your leadership. Always remember the fable of the Emperor's new clothes." (Starratt, p. 350)

I was very impressed by the skill with which this school leader dealt with parental resistance. She told me about one parent described by the previous principal and the teachers as a real nuisance. This mother of five had been a thorn in the side of more than one administrator in the school: she was always in the building, often complaining about one thing or another. Laura told me, "I just had to do something proactive; she was driving us all foolish." So, Laura put the parent to work as a volunteer, reasoning that if she were going to be in the school everyday, she might as well be doing something useful. After several months, the parent became the school's strongest advocate. She decided that something needed to be done about the significant number of students in the school whose families could not afford a Thanksgiving dinner. Within a month she had organized other parents to provide a sit-down turkey dinner for all 500 children and invited guests. As the result of the principal's attitude and actions, a person who had been an annoyance to everyone became a positive presence in the school, contributing to making the school a better place to work and learn.

While every school is different, I think there are lessons to be learned from the experiences of one school leader:

- Time spent listening to students and parents is well spent; it pays dividends in the development of positive and productive working relationships.
- A principal can effect changes in school culture through clarity of vision, consistency of responses, and patience.

- There will always be parents who do not agree with what the leader is doing. A focus on them can blind a leader to the many parents who are supportive.

When a parent or small group of parents demand too much time and contribute negative energy to the school, a good solution is to put the complainers to work. This not only redirects the energy, but it also can help the parent(s) gain insights into the issues the school is facing and may lead to more positive support for the school's efforts.

Happy students make for happy parents, as this parent summed it up: "The kids are very happy here. It's good for self-esteem especially…. Now that I see this school and the way that they work with the kids and get them involved with things, I really feel they are doing a good job."

Involved Communities

Community schools — those that are true community centres, open beyond school hours and built on extensive partnerships — have been the focus of extensive research.

Researchers Epstein and Salinas make a distinction between professional learning communities, which they define as having an emphasis on the professional staff working collaboratively, and school learning communities, which involve students, parents, and community partners as well. There is research (Epstein; Henderson & Mapp; Sheldon) documenting how organized programs of school/community partnerships "improve schools, strengthen families, invigorate community support, and increase student achievement and success" (Epstein & Salinas, p. 12). The Coalition for Community Schools in the United States (Blank, p. 63) found

- significant and widespread gains in academic achievement and in essential areas of non-academic development
- increased family stability and greater family involvement with schools.
- increased teacher satisfaction and more positive school environments
- better use of school buildings and increased security and pride in neighborhoods

In today's society, where there are relatively few stay-at-home parents and many families experience significant economic challenges, there is a need for schools to diversify the ways in which parents can participate in the school. As well, schools need to be sensitive to the growing number of families in which parents speak no or limited English. In a national study in the United States, Dauber and Epstein found that the best predictor of parent involvement was what the school did to promote it. What the school did was far more important than parents' income, educational level, race, or previous school volunteer experiences in predicting whether a parent would be involved with the school.

Schools can promote several types of parental involvement:

- Parenting
- Communicating
- Volunteering
- Learning at Home
- Decision Making
- Collaborating with the Community

As schools work towards engaging parents more meaningfully, it can be helpful to engage in periodic self-evaluation. Schools can draw upon these reflections in setting priorities and monitoring progress. Examples of the kinds of questions that might frame this process are included in reproducible form on pages 38–39.

Involving Parents and Community Members

The Center on School, Family, and Community Partnerships at John's Hopkins University (http://www.csos.jhu.edu/p2000/center.htm) has an extensive list of publications related to parent and community involvement. The web site also provides links to other useful resources.

The North Central Regional Educational Laboratory has a number of useful resources and links to other sites related to families and communities on its web site at http:www.ncrel.org/sdrs/areas/issues/envrnmnt/famncomm

Epstein et al recommend that schools broaden parent involvement by including as many of the six following types of parental involvement as possible.

- Parenting: this is two-way learning in which schools provide assistance to families in improving parenting skills, but also seek better understanding of families' cultures and hopes for their children.
- Communicating: this involves the creation of two-way communication in as many forms as possible.
- Volunteering: well-organized volunteer programs can meaningfully involve parents in working in the school.
- Learning at Home: parents can be involved in assisting students with learning at home, especially if teachers design homework in which parents can be meaningful participants.
- Decision Making: schools can include parents through formal structures such as advisory councils, but also through committees, parent organizations, and problem solving around specific issues.
- Collaborating with the Community: the school can play a coordinating role in mobilizing community resources and developing partnerships with agencies, businesses, and civic and cultural groups. Schools can make programs of community service an integral part of the curriculum at all age levels.

There are many possibilities for action within the six types of parental involvement described above. Key to the success of any kind of parent involvement is the principal's role in establishing and sustaining a school climate in which the participation of parents is welcomed and celebrated. Principals need to set expectations for teachers that include establishing two-way communication with parents and inviting them to be partners in learning. Ways of involving parents range from small changes that can easily be incorporated to elaborate educational and volunteer programs. The following represent only a small sample of the many ways in which schools can enhance the role of parents and community members.

Parenting

The simplest way in which schools can positively influence parenting practices is through the day-to-day interactions that teachers and administrators have with parents. In the course of discussions regarding the learning of individual students, teachers or administrators can make suggestions regarding ways parents can better support their children or deal with specific issues such as discipline. School personnel can also use these opportunities to extend their understanding of the family values and culture, thus creating more coherence between students' home and school experiences. Schools can also

- provide workshops on topics of interest to parents
- create a resource library with books, pamphlets, and videotapes related to parenting
- draw upon the resources of community agencies to assist individual or small groups of parents with specific issues, such as behavior, school phobia, or other social-emotional problems.

Communication

Before sending home a letter or other communication, ask yourself and several trusted readers, "How is this letter or newsletter likely to be perceived? Is the communication personal or impersonal, inviting or uninviting? Will this letter evoke a response?"

As I observed through my research, a principal who keeps the door open to staff and parents develops trusting relationships that greatly enhance the school community. It is also important to monitor written communication.

Teachers have an important role to play in keeping communication lines open. When teachers phone parents regularly to touch base and to report on what is going well with a child, the lines of communication are already open if there is a need to address a problem. Teachers, too, need to monitor written communication. Professional development related to effective oral and written communication may be very helpful to them.

Additional suggestions for keeping lines of communication open include the following:

- Teachers can send home samples of student work regularly and invite parental comments.
- When working through issues such as student behavior, teachers and parents can communicate daily or weekly through a journal.
- Schools can enhance the impact of newsletters by including contributions from students and parents.
- Schools can support communication with all families through the use of language translators where needed.
- Teachers and administrators can schedule conferences with parents at intervals during the year. Some schools have developed student-led conferences, during which teachers, parents, and students discuss the child's progress and learning goals (more extensive description of these conferences is included in Chapter 6).
- In communities in which technology is available to most families, schools can use e-mail or web-based communications tools.
- School personnel can move parent-teacher meetings, special events, and other gatherings into community centres or other locations that may be more inviting and accessible to parents than the school.

Volunteering

Some schools have established mentoring programs in which they draw upon community volunteers to establish one-to-one relationships that respond to students' individual interests or needs.

Many types of volunteerism are possible in a school. Individual teachers can draw upon parents and community members to assist with preparation of materials, to read and write with students, to oversee special activities, and to chaperone school trips. Schools use volunteers to help in the school library, to raise funds, and to assist with school-wide projects. Parents and community members with particular talents may conduct workshops with children, assist with extracurricular activities, or lead school clubs.

Many schools use volunteers extensively and establish organizational supports for these programs. These organizational supports include

- the use of experienced volunteers to coordinate volunteer programs and to recruit new people
- wide distribution of information regarding a broad range of volunteer opportunities in the school
- yearly surveys of the community to identify potential volunteers and to gather information regarding expertise
- active recruitment of volunteers through newsletters, word-of-mouth, and efforts of individual teachers within their own classes

- staff development for teachers on how to use volunteers effectively
- training programs for volunteers
- designated spaces in the school for volunteers to meet and to store resources used in their volunteer activities
- recognition for volunteers, such as yearly volunteer teas, acknowledgment in school newsletters, certificates, and thank-you letters.

Learning at Home

Many elementary schools provide sessions on how children learn literacy and math, and on how parents can help. Workshops for parents of older students might focus on study strategies or ways to support learners who are struggling.

Making links between home and school in relation to students' academic learning is one of the most important ways in which parent involvement influences student achievement. Inviting parents to visit the classroom to see the curriculum in action opens the door for parents to become active partners in their children's learning. Schools can also plan workshops designed to enhance parents' understanding of the curriculum so that they are better able to support their children at home.

Supporting students directly with academic tasks may not be possible for parents for whom there are language barriers, whose educational backgrounds are not strong, or who lack time because of work schedules or home responsibilities. To ensure the active involvement of all parents, teachers need to consider the kinds of tasks they are assigning for homework. These tasks should not put the parent in the role of teacher but, instead, purposefully engage students in interacting with their parents or guardians:

- Students might be asked to interview a parent or grandparent about aspects of schooling in their day, or about their work.
- Students might read with and to a parent or older sibling, or families might watch a television program together and respond to it with guidelines from the teacher.
- Parents might help with a simple science experiment using things found in the kitchen.
- Students and parents might work through goal setting at home with guidelines from the school.
- Schools or individual teachers can develop lists of inexpensive or free community activities that relate to curriculum content (museums, art galleries, concerts, films, nature walks, readings by authors, etc.) or that enhance learning potential (family fitness, participation in sports, etc.).

Schools and individual teachers need to keep parents informed about the curriculum through curriculum nights, newsletters, and communications from individual teachers. Moving beyond information giving, teachers can invite parents to participate in discussions regarding ways parents can help at home, drawing on parents' prior experiences and asking for their suggestions. If these discussions take place at curriculum meetings, the teacher can facilitate the dissemination of ideas to all parents of students in the class. Newsletters might have a spot for parents to send in suggestions. Interactive web sites are ideal for ongoing conversations related to the curriculum. These discussions may well lead to the participation of more parents in the classroom for the purpose of sharing their expertise related to an area of the curriculum.

Decision Making

In highly decentralized structures, parent councils may have wide-ranging authority, including hiring principals and staff, controlling budgets, and having accountability. In many jurisdictions, however, these councils are advisory, and authority for school operations rests with the school principal.

The majority of current school governance models include formal structures for involving parents in decision making through various kinds of parent councils. Parent advisory councils and parents in general usually have an active role to play in school improvement processes.

Ensuring that all parents have equal opportunities for participation in these important activities is a challenge for principals. Participation requires a commitment of time as well as the confidence to work with the professionals in the school. It is usually easier to attract parents with higher levels of education and income, so administrators have to be proactive in recruiting representation from all the communities that the school serves. Building trusting relationships through informal interactions with parents is the best way to make them feel confident about becoming part of a parent council or school improvement team. Teachers can be involved in encouraging parents of the children in their classes to become involved. Where feasible, arranging child care, translation services, stipends to cover transportation costs, or carpools can be helpful.

When I spoke to the parents in Laura's school as part of my research, they expressed great willingness to be involved in decision making in the school. They wanted to be able to provide their perspectives on issues that affected their children. There was some frustration with what the parents perceived to be cumbersome processes that guided improvement planning. The formal structures seemed to get in the way of participation that was meaningful from the parents' perspectives. Clearly, if parents are going to be involved in making decisions, there need to be parameters and processes established. The last thing a principal needs is a group of parents trying to help run the school without a framework for their involvement. If school leaders value authentic parent participation, however, they need to design structures and processes that provide the necessary direction but that also foster productive, shared decision making.

To enhance the authentic involvement of parents, schools leaders need to look beyond formal structures, such as councils and school improvement committees, and consider other ways in which parents can share in making decisions. Some of these include,

- parent participation on staff/community short-term committees with a limited scope and clear objectives; for example, making decisions about how to spend funds raised by a parent-teacher organization to support the curriculum
- involvement of parents in the development of school policies, through focus meetings to invite input and through response to drafts of policies prepared by professional staff
- distribution of surveys to gather parental input on curriculum, operational matters, or specific issues on which decisions have to be made

Collaborating with the Community

Historically, schools have been institutions that bind communities together. Today it is often the school that assists parents in gaining access to essential health and community services. The movement to develop full-service schools has been ongoing for several decades in many constituencies.

The development of full-service schools is dependent on the will of government agencies to transcend bureaucratic boundaries in order to provide services

Full-service schools become the location for health, mental health, and social service agency programs, giving community members easier access to psychological counseling; medical and dental services; social assistance and other community services; and parent education. The coordination of services for families through these structures has proven extremely beneficial to the clients as well as to the agencies involved.

in a coherent way within the community. While such institutional collaboration may be beyond what is possible in many communities, schools can still play an important role in making connections across community agencies on behalf of the children that they serve. Some ways in which school leaders can facilitate these connections are as follows:

- Develop close working relationships with the people from community agencies and organizations that serve the local community. The principal should make contact with these individuals, telling them about the school and emphasizing the desire to work together on behalf of children, youth, and families.
- As much as is possible within governing policy frameworks, invite community groups to locate their activities in the school.
- Draw upon community groups to provide parenting sessions, to mentor students, to contribute their expertise, and to assist with special events. Seek out visual artists, musicians, writers, craftspersons, athletes, and others with skills and talents, and invite them to participate actively in the life of the school. Investigate sources of funding to support such participation.
- Develop service learning programs, through which students give back to the community by volunteering to provide a range of services that support individuals and groups as well as to improve the community as a whole.
- Seek out relationships with colleges and universities, inviting the participation of faculty in professional development experiences for teachers (including action research, see page 21) and in support of the curriculum. In turn, be open to providing placement for student teachers and to working with academics in research projects.
- Involve students in learning more about their local communities as part of the curriculum across grade levels.

Asking Questions

School leaders who truly want to enhance the involvement of students, parents, and other community members need to actively seek their input and act upon what they learn. This can be done through informal interactions, or more formally through short questionnaires or surveys. Sample questionnaires for use with students, parents, and community members are included in reproducible form on pages 38 to 45.

Students

When I asked students to describe what they would include in a video about the school, it yielded a wealth of insights about how they viewed the people in the building and the place in which they were learning. This might be an excellent question for a school leader to pose to groups of students from time to time as a way of monitoring student perceptions.

School leaders can develop a questionnaire to monitor student perceptions (see Principal's Questionnaire for Students on pages 40–41). They might draw upon research tools developed by Nemerowicz and Rosi as part of a study on education for leadership and social responsibility. The researchers asked students to "draw a picture of leadership" and then invited them to talk about their pictures in one-to-one interviews. In these discussions, the interviewers asked the children to define leadership, to share their feelings about leadership, and to give advice to leaders. Such a tool, used informally by a leader, has the potential to give a principal honest feedback on efforts to enact collaborative leadership. It also can provide insights into whether or not students see their teachers or themselves as leaders.

Nemerowicz and Rosi offer the following suggestions for enhancing the leadership capacities of students, thus contributing to the development of collaboration in the school:

- Make the topic of leadership a more direct part of curriculum and conversation.
- Introduce the idea of a "common good."
- Increase collaborative learning opportunities and reinforce the association between leadership and problem-finding and solving.
- Analyze the way decisions are made in the school and in the family.
- Involve adults — teachers and parents — as partners in learning with the child.
- Point out examples of leadership in the world beyond politics and government, and provide opportunities for student to experience and practice leadership.
- Develop in children an awareness of the importance of active, participatory leadership.
- Discuss with the individual child his or her leadership potential.
- Provide more information about the leadership contributions of women in all arenas.
- Reinforce interpersonal skills for their importance in leadership.
- Allow time for coaches and teachers to reflect on what and how they are teaching about leadership.

Parents

School leaders can develop questionnaires to seek parental input (see Principal's Questionnaire for Parents on pages 42–43). In order to ensure that all parents are able to participate, principals may need to work with community groups or the district to have these questionnaires translated into several languages. Schools may also want to offer parents the opportunity to attend meetings where they can provide their input orally in order to include those with literacy challenges; they might consider putting the questionnaires online for parents who have access to technology. Dauber and Epstein suggest that a questionnaire include questions that cover the following:

- parent attitudes towards their children's school
- the school subjects that parents want to know more about.
- how frequently parents are involved in different ways in their children's education
- how well school programs and teacher practices inform and involve them in their children's education
- workshop topics they would select
- the times of day parents prefer for meetings or conferences at school
- how much time their children spend on homework, and whether parents help
- background information about parents' education, work, and family size

Gaining input from adults in the community, beyond parents of students, can be challenging. Individuals in the community who are not parents can be invited to participate on school advisory councils (in some constituencies this is a requirement). Schools can also distribute questionnaires beyond the school, describing school activities and inviting participation (see Principal's Questionnaire for Community Members on pages 44–45). If school activities such as fundraising or service learning require the involvement of community agencies or businesses, it is a courtesy to invite their participation during the planning stages. Such openness is likely to enhance the possibility of garnering support, rather than resistance.

The Larger Educational System

Under Laura's leadership, the school was focused on improving student learning. The many badly coordinated demands from outside distracted, frustrated, and sapped energies.

Notwithstanding the moves to reframe definitions of leadership as broadly relational, involving complex interactions among internal and external players, schools today seem to be primarily on the receiving end of initiatives, mandates, and regulations that are generated externally. I documented this perspective extensively in my own research and made the argument, based on what I learned from the school case study, that such uni-directional exercising of authority undermined many of the efforts the school was making to function as a professional community.

At the time that I conducted the case study, the district was two years into a restructuring and amalgamation of several boards. Laura mentioned the district a number of times in my conversations with her. I constructed the following poetic transcript by reading across interviews with her, identifying places where she talked about the district.

POST-AMALGAMATION SYNDROME:
THE PRINCIPAL

You've heard it all before
Isolation
They feel disconnected.
As a school you come together
And come to the realization,
We're it.
And we have to depend upon each other
In this building.
Each department is so focused
On their own agenda.
They're so territorial.
They believe
Their memo is the
Only memo
Going out.
Come to a meeting.
Come for information.
Meeting.
People are meetinged to death.

Every time you turn around
There is a new curriculum guide.
And there's time,
That four-letter word.
People's heads are just spinning

My biggest question is,
How do we make the connection
Between
What's written on those pages
And what shape it takes in the classroom?
It's just huge

The supervisor told the teachers,
Learn this.
Know it.
Memorize it.
Practise it.
Whatever.
But if teachers don't make that connection…
Until you can connect it
Or help them make that connection,
It's not going to happen.

You have to have a plan
Everybody else has a plan.
That's how Central Office works.
The Department is asking,
Where is your plan?
How do you know if your schools
Are on track?
It's an accountability thing;
They need to tell someone
We're actually doing it.
Those Central Office people
Are dying a slow death.
I can't pass judgment
On Central Office.
I think people are getting sick.
They're really getting sick.
And if they're not,
Five years from now
They're going to go to their doctor
And say,
You know, I have this facial tic…
Or I'm not sleeping…
Or I'm not eating…
It's just too much.

This poem captures a moment in the history of this organization when things were at their most confusing. Yet, in my experience, it has *always* been difficult to orchestrate mutually supportive relationships across levels of the organization, in effect extending the professional learning community beyond the school. This becomes increasingly difficult the larger and more complex the organization.

Research that is related to the role of systems in enhancing student learning documents the need for systems to become less bureaucratic and hierarchical.

Most of the responsibility for changing how districts and other external agencies work with schools lies beyond school leaders. While systems have the responsibility to set expectations and to monitor the performance of schools, the role is primarily a "connecting" (Rhodes) one, in which there is a shift from regulating to supporting the development of capacities within schools through professional development and appropriate resource allocation. Studies of Local Education Authorities in the UK (Riley, Docking & Rowles) showed that "the 'ethos' of an authority carried rather more weight with respondents than the quality of its specific services" (p. 119). The researchers identified five factors that contributed to positive ethos, as follows: "gives value for money, consults effectively with teachers, 'puts its money where its mouth is', is highly supportive of heads and teachers, and plans successfully for the educational needs of the community as a whole" (p. 119). The respondents in the study put emphasis on the nature and quality of relationships. The most effective systems worked to bind the community together rather than contributing to its fragmentation.

Packer conducted a very informative study of school reform in a small community called Willow Run in Michigan, where top-down, external initiatives competed with the efforts of those at the local level to shape school change efforts in response to their self-identified priorities. In the concluding chapter, Packer discusses the messages of evaluation reports and summaries published at the end of the state's five-year reform effort. One of the findings was that "the educational system has 'limited capacity' to implement change" (p. 275). Packer comments that this is one way for the reformers to absolve themselves of blame for the disappointing results of the systemic reform. It might also, however, be an indication "that the systemic reform initiative has discovered the people who live in the system" (p.275). That is, the evaluators acknowledged the complexities of local school contexts and made recommendations regarding the need to change roles and relationships. Packer's final comment in the book, "Willow Run knew this" (p. 276), echoes what I learned through my case study.

I found that *both* the school and the district lacked the capacity they needed to respond to the diverse range of students in the system. In fact, the school demonstrated far *greater* capacities than the district for enacting changes that enhanced the learning context for students. Earlier, I discussed how principals enhance relationships within schools through mutual capacity building. The same kind of processes, in which all levels of the system — province, district, and school — positively affect their individual and collective capacities, is a more productive way of thinking about the relationships between internal and external leaders. Capacity building is not a matter of each level of the hierarchy improving the capacities of the one below it, but of each influencing and learning from the other. Such a perspective acknowledges the complex, relational nature of leadership.

While those external to the school may not always be willing to listen to what schools have to teach them, that should not stop principals from making their voices heard.

Principals can enact principles of mutual capacity building by reaching beyond the school to inform others (communities, businesses, the larger system, and government) about their needs and priorities. By the same token, principals also need to learn from the external environment, developing insights into *how* systems work so that they can make those systems work *for* their schools. They need to be aware of societal changes that affect their schools and to understand the political contexts in which they work.

A recent study (McGinn) with ten principals nominated by others as dynamic leaders showed that "social and political acumen" are essential characteristics of effective principals in current contexts. Principals with social acumen are skilled at communications and relationship building; those with political acumen have knowledge of structures and relationships, and are able to use that knowledge to benefit the school.

Chapters 5 and 6 discuss specific ways in which principals can address external expectations regarding school management and accountability. School leaders better position themselves to do so when they work proactively with the larger organization, focusing on enhancing the capacities of that organization to support their schools. Not in any way underestimating the difficulties in making changes "from the bottom-up," I suggest that, as a principal, you consider the following:

"You need to go beyond the classroom focus and the school focus. I need to go beyond and see the big picture, and, you know, I strategize a little on how to get everyone by." (McGinn, p. 8).

- See your school as part of the larger organization, whether that is a school district or some other governance structure. While it might be tempting to try to close the doors and "cocoon," as one of the teachers in Laura's school described it, schools need to be aware of the external context.
- Participate in professional development outside the school and encourage teachers to do so. Within the school, discuss how these experiences relate to what you are working towards as a learning community.
- Clarify your internal priorities and communicate them to the larger system. Demonstrate through these communications that the school is a well-functioning professional learning community focused on student learning.
- Make demands on the system for human and material resources to support your priorities. When a school is clear about where it is going, it is better able to tell the larger organization what it needs in terms of staffing, materials and equipment, and professional development. You may not always get what you want and need, but you can be assertive in making requests.
- Invite school-district staff, other external administrators, and elected board members or trustees to the school. Demonstrate the ways that the school is working to enhance student learning. Discuss with them your priorities and needs.
- Create and sustain positive working relationships with those in support positions in the bureaucracy. When you interact professionally and respectfully with those you contact in the larger organization, you build networks you can draw upon when you need assistance from the system.
- If the school is part of a system governed by an elected school board, attend meetings periodically and read minutes of meetings to stay informed about policy issues.

- Look for critical friends in the system. These can be principal colleagues or district leaders with whom you develop open and trusting relationships that allow for honest dialogue about your practices. You can ask advice and seek feedback regarding ways to improve. In some organizations, groups of critical friends meet regularly to examine practices collaboratively and openly.

School Self-Evaluation: Parent and Community Involvement

1. In what ways are teachers and the school as a whole currently involving parents and other community members?

2. How do the practices differ across the grades? What specific ways of partnering are working well?

3. How might teachers at each grade level improve and/or expand their current practices?

4. What are our long-term goals for partnering with parents and community? What kinds of practices would we like to see in place in three to five years?

5. Which families and communities are currently involved? If there are individual families or particular communities served by the school who are not currently involved, how might we reach out to them?

6. Is there a cost to any of the improvements in partnering that we want to make? If so, how will we fund our efforts?

7. What strategies do we have for ongoing sharing and communication among students, parents, and teachers in regard to our partnering efforts? How can we learn from each other? What evidence will we collect to document progress towards our long-term goals?

Principal's Questionnaire for Students

(These questions can be read to students who are unable to read them independently; students can respond orally or through drawing.)

1. What do you like best about this school? (Draw or write your answer)

2. What do like least about this school? (Draw or write your answer)

3. If you could change one thing about this school, what would it be?

4. Do you enjoy coming to school? Why or why not?

5. Do you feel safe in this school? Why or why not?

6. Draw or write about the most interesting thing you learned this week.

7. What does the principal do to make this school a good place to learn? (Draw or write your answer)

8. How does the principal help you?

9. What other ways could the principal help you?

10. Is there anything else that you would like the principal to know?

Principal's Questionnaire for Parents

As principal of the school, I am interesting in knowing how we are doing. I would appreciate your completing the following brief questionnaire and returning it to the school.

Number of your children who attend the school: _____

1. Is this school meeting the learning needs of your child? If we are not, please let us know how we can do better.

2. What is this school doing well?

3. In what areas are improvements needed?

4. Do you have suggestions for how we might improve in the areas you have identified?

5. Do you find the administrators and teachers easy to contact and supportive? If not, how can we improve?

6. What can I, as the principal, do to make the school experience better for you and your child?

7. Do you feel that you are well informed about your child's program?

   ❏ Yes   ❏ No

8. What areas of the curriculum would you like to know more about?

9. If the school were to offer workshops on curriculum, other aspects of education, or parenting, what topics would be of interest?

10. What time of day is most convenient for you to attend school meetings, parent conferences, or workshops?

    ❏ During the day   ❏ Late afternoon   ❏ Evening

Principal's Questionnaire for Community Members

As principal of a school that serves your community, I am interested in knowing how we can work together. We want community members to feel that this is their school as well, and we need your support to create the very best learning environment possible for our students. I would appreciate your taking the time to complete this short questionnaire.

Please indicate your role in the community. Check all that apply

❏ Resident   ❏ Business owner/manager
❏ Employee in local business   ❏ Administrator or employee in a community agency
❏ Administrator or employee of a public or private post-secondary institution
❏ Other: _____

1. Have you had any involvement with our school in the past? If so, in what ways?

2. From your knowledge of our school and students, what are we doing well? How might we improve in our efforts to be positive members of this community?

3. From time to time, our school is engaged in fundraising within the community.

   Are you aware of these efforts?   ❏ Yes   ❏ No

   Have these efforts had a direct impact on you? ❏ Yes   ❏ No

   Has this been positive ❏ or negative ❏ ?

Do you have suggestions for how our fundraising efforts might be improved?

Please feel free to add any other comments.

_____

_____

_____

_____

_____

_____

_____

An Invitation to Become Involved

Our programs are greatly enhanced when community members participate in our classroom and school activities. Please check any of the forms of participation listed below you would be willing to consider.

❏ Volunteer in classroom or school

❏ Mentoring students

❏ One-time visits to share skills, talents, or experiences

❏ Participation in career days

❏ Other: _____

If you are interested in becoming involved with our school, please provide your name, address, and contact information below and return this sheet separately from the questionnaire.

- -

Name: _____

Address: _____

_____

_____

Phone (w) _____ (h)_____

E-mail: _____

CHAPTER 3   Schools as Diverse Multicultural
            Communities

Overlapping and shifting categories of race, culture, ethnicity, gender, sexual identity, social class, ability, and other forms of difference make grappling with issues of diversity increasingly complex.

When I was enrolled in a teacher education program in the late 1960s in the United States, I learned about diversity through the tumultuous events of the Civil Rights movement. My student teaching assignment was in a school in an upper-middleclass suburb of Boston to which African-American students from the inner city were bussed through forced integration. I observed firsthand the bitterness and anger within both communities. I also became aware that the differences that created the barriers between the communities were in social class as well as race. Nearly forty years later, efforts to achieve equality for African-American and African-Canadian people continue within a context in which diversity now encompasses many forms of difference. Schools, as microcosms of society, are sites in which the complexities of diversity become evident, as administrators and teachers attempt to respond sensitively and appropriately to the students and families with whom they interact.

With the increase in immigration to North America from all over the world, schools face the challenge of learning about the home languages and cultures of students and families from many different countries. At the same time, schools must design programs and services that help these children and their families become part of the community and develop the skills and knowledge they need in order to be fully participating citizens of their new country. Where, at one time, immigrants mostly settled in larger, urban centres, in recent years there has been more immigration to smaller cities and towns, and to rural communities. Provinces (such as Nova Scotia) with declining populations are actively seeking immigrants. Therefore, the cultural and linguistic diversity of school populations is increasing in many different types of communities.

A school community that enacts inclusive practices prepares students to contribute to the development of larger communities that create spaces for diversity, both valuing and celebrating differences.

Whether or not a school currently serves such a population, all of today's students will be living and working in a global society. Schools have a central role to play in expanding students' awareness of the multiple ways in which different peoples of the world think, believe, and act, based upon their histories and cultures. As expressed eloquently by Hargreaves (2003), globalization can result in increasing fear and terrorism — evident in world events — or there is an alternative response

> ...for those who prosper most from the knowledge economy to share its bounty more evenly with poorer groups in their own society, and with less-developed nations beyond it. It is to create a cosmopolitan rather than conquering vision of a globalized knowledge society that is inclusive rather than exclusive in its logic. (p. 48)

The development of a cosmopolitan vision begins in school, where students learn respect and responsibility for each other. Further, through a curriculum that enhances their understanding of the histories and cultures of diverse groups, they expand that sense of responsibility beyond the walls of the school.

Leadership as Critical Practice

When schools envision themselves as collaborative learning communities and incorporate the kinds of practices discussed in the first two chapters of this book, they enhance their capacities to include a diverse range of learners and their families as participating members. To become truly responsive to this diversity, however, collaborative learning communities need to confront the reality that societal inequalities based upon differences in race, culture, gender, language, ability, sexual identity, age, and other factors influence and are represented in school contexts. The work of leadership in such contexts involves fostering what researcher Furman calls "communities of otherness," in which differences are recognized and accepted. Starratt suggests that leaders need to make schools "learning laboratories for democratic living" and to create structures and processes that provide maximum possibilities for adults and children with diverse perspectives to contribute to the life and work of the school.

Leadership of this kind is a form of critical practice, bringing issues of social justice and equity to the fore. When leaders take up their work as critical practice, they make differences a focus in their attempt to transform social inequalities. Corson suggests that administrators in settings of great diversity need to practice "emancipatory leadership" in order to guard against inadvertently perpetuating injustices. Such leaders acknowledge that they lack the expertise to represent the interests of diverse groups in decision making, and they institute practices through which those groups can represent themselves. Within critical conceptions of leadership there is also a commitment to developing more inclusionary practices in leadership itself, through greater access to leadership positions for people who have historically been marginalized.

Critical leadership practices must work from complex conceptions of diversity, such as that offered by Nieto, who defines culture as

> ...the ever-changing values, traditions, social and political relationships, and worldview created, shared, and transformed by a group of people bound together by a combination of factors that include a common history, geographic location, language, social class, and religion. (p. 48)

Several attributes of culture described by Nieto help to show the connection between culture and learning: "Culture is dynamic; multi-faceted; embedded in context, influenced by social, economic, and political factors; created and socially constructed; learned; and dialectical" (p. 49).

A good place for leaders to begin to become more responsive to diversity in their schools is by developing deeper insights into their own cultural beliefs and practices. Most of us rarely, if ever, critically examine our own "values, traditions, social and political relationships, and worldview." Instead, we assume that it's just the way the world is supposed to be. Leaders with expanded self-knowledge are better positioned to detect their own biases, to understand how the diverse students and families in the school community view the world and express those worldviews through their cultures. Leaders should engage all those who work in the school in similar processes, so that all develop the cultural sensitivity to enable

Through critical leadership practices, administrators move beyond the superficial approaches to multiculturalism that limit attention to diversity to special events focusing on food, fashion, and other visible aspects of cultures.

them to maximize the learning of all students. Such leaders bring social justice and equity to the fore through their daily interactions and through the ways in which they invite participation. They also work with teachers to ensure that the curriculum not only reflects and represents diverse cultures, but also engages children in examining how power relationships work in the society in which they live.

Becoming More Responsive to Diversity

North Central Regional Laboratory web-site includes a helpful critical issues discussion paper *Addressing Literacy Needs in Culturally and Linguistically Diverse Classrooms.* The article can be accessed at http:// www.ncrel.org/sdrs/areas/issues/ content/cntareas/reading/li400.htm

Although the school in which I conducted my case study did not serve a visibly multicultural community, the principal's leadership practices reflected her understanding that her school was, nevertheless, diverse. Laura responded proactively to that diversity in a number of ways.
Responding proactively to diversity includes

- developing respect, care, and social responsibility
- changing beliefs, attitudes, and expectations
- expanding knowledge and understanding
- constructing culturally relevant teaching
- developing close working relationships with families and community members

Developing Respect, Care, and Social Responsibility

A section of the school improvement plan that described the social/demographic context of the school included an extensive list of social issues: high unemployment; increased poverty; racism, classism, and sexism; economic differences in communities served by the school; and increased violence. Laura told me that it was slow going to lead staff and community to make connections between these broader issues and the problems with student behavior and learning in the school. In order to help others make those connections, she brought explicit attention to social justice and equity through her focus on peace education, conflict resolution, the development of mutual respect, and the enhancement of student self-responsibility.

During the year I conducted my case study, the school held its second peace conference. Reflecting on this in one of the interviews, Laura said, "Last year it was just to raise awareness, more or less, and get children introduced to the language. And then this year, we were able to do more in-depth things." Among the fourteen workshops open to students in Grades 3 through 6 were several with a specific focus on social justice. For example, a race relations consultant talked about racial name-calling and bullying. In other sessions, teachers from neighbouring schools led discussions on social justice issues in the classroom. A community leader focused on the causes of bullying, and the peer mediators from the school presented a session on conflict resolution.

In our conversations, Laura consistently returned to the theme of respect for all children. She left no doubt about her belief that adults should educate children rather than use their power to punish them:

> Teachers have said that a quick fix is to perhaps yell at a child or point a finger in a child's face, and to me it's demeaning; I have difficulty with that. I don't think that's supportive for a child and I don't think that a child learns. A child doesn't learn anything from that kind of situation except [that] "big eats small." And I've sort of gotten on my soapbox with staff and talked about "big eats small," and all the children learn when we yell at kids is [that] big people yell at little people and when I get big then I can do it and I can yell at little people. And it just perpetuates that cycle.

Changing Beliefs, Attitudes, and Expectations

Principals in schools that serve multicultural, multiracial populations face even greater challenges than Laura in creating and sustaining a supportive context for students and families. Teachers may, through lack of understanding of diverse cultures and of the needs of children who do not speak the language of instruction, believe that these children are less-capable learners. Sometimes racist or ethnocentric attitudes underlie teacher beliefs, and the school leader must take proactive steps, setting clear expectations for staff and providing necessary professional development. Teachers may also lack the knowledge required to shape instruction that helps students bridge the gap between their prior knowledge and the new learning that is required for them to be successful. Teachers' expectations, communicated both verbally and non-verbally, have a powerful effect on students' beliefs about themselves and on their behavior and performance. It is important that educators convey their confidence in children's ability to learn and then set high expectations, supported by culturally relevant teaching.

A recent article in the *Christian Science Monitor* (Weingarten) demonstrated how powerfully teachers' misconceptions affect students. The article focuses on how teachers often overlook quiet children or consider them less able than their more extroverted peers. Focusing on controlling the behavior of more vocal and disruptive students, teachers spend less time with children who seek less attention. Many cultures (particularly some Asian cultures) value quiet, restrained, and reflective behavior, and foster these traits in their children. The parent of two boys with Narragansett Indian heritage told the reporter that it's a difficulty Native Americans have coped with for decades: "Native learning is that you are supposed to be contemplative and reflective, thoughtful, and you aren't supposed to be competitive." In public school, educators judged her boys as lacking in social skills, so she moved her children to a private school more attuned to their needs. A teacher interviewed for the article commented on how important is for teachers to learn how to adjust classroom instruction so that the quiet children, many of whom are from other cultures, have a chance to participate. Strategies include small-group instruction, open-ended questions that encourage contemplation and deeper thinking, valuing quiet students' strengths, and social codes that set expectations for full participation.

Administrators and teachers need to be personally committed to achieving equity for all students and to believe that they can make a difference in students' lives.

Expanding Knowledge and Understanding

Both administrators and teachers need to expand their knowledge and understanding related to working with diverse populations. A number of researchers have identified the kinds of knowledge needed by educators; Haberman and Post include the following in their list:

- self-knowledge and self-acceptance: understanding and valuing one's own culture
- relationship skills: understanding how to work with those different from oneself, demonstrating care and respect
- community knowledge: insights into the cultural heritages of children and families; understanding and appreciation of diverse backgrounds and lifestyles
- empathy: ability to "walk in another's shoes"
- awareness of how culture influences learning, and of the possible sources of conflict between values of cultural groups and dominant values of the school
- understanding of how to make curriculum relevant and how to engage students in sustained efforts
- anti-violence and anti-racist strategies
- capacity for ongoing reflection and change within an unpredictable environment (many different cultures and languages, high level of turnover in student population, etc.)

In many respects, this type of teaching reflects current insights into how all children learn: students need to be actively engaged in constructing meaning within a context in which there are a broad range of individual and group learning experiences.

Constructing Culturally Relevant Teaching

Drawing on their knowledge and understanding of diversity, educators are better able to respond through appropriate teaching. Teachers help children to build upon their prior knowledge and provide extensive opportunities for social interaction. Beyond that, in more culturally and linguistically diverse classrooms, there is a need to

- include a wide range of multicultural literature and ensure that cultural groups are accurately represented in all texts and materials.
- ensure that the curriculum reflects the contributions and perspectives of the different ethnocultural groups that make up society.
- help students learn classroom expectations, routines, and patterns, which may be very different from those previously experienced.
- build in instructional scaffolding that helps students link the school curriculum to the cultural resources that they bring to learning.
- observe and learn from the students, identifying preferred learning styles and task preferences, so that instruction better matches students' needs and interests.
- draw upon families and community members as a resource (in many communities, multicultural associations can provide insights into diverse cultures and contribute to the curriculum).
- accept and value students' home languages while engaging in a process through which they acquire proficiency in the dominant language.
- learn about children's home languages and cultural differences in communication patterns.

- value alternative ways of knowing, such as oral traditions and the arts through which many cultures make meaning; help children connect these with dominant forms of school literacies.
- create a classroom context in which cross-cultural exchanges are the norm, so that children learn with and from each other, enriching all.

Developing Close Working Relationships with Families and Community Members

Schools need to find ways to engage parents, caregivers, and other community members in students' education and in the life of the school, overcoming language and cultural barriers when necessary. It is essential for administrators and teachers to enhance their knowledge of how learning occurs at home in different linguistic and cultural groups. They need to examine preconceived notions about such topics as home literacy; for example, Auerbach found many educators held untrue assumptions about families' lack of interest in their children's education. Other research documents the rich variety of language uses and literacy events across many different cultures. Schools need to reach out to families and develop collaborative approaches to learning, drawing upon the resources that families bring rather than expecting them to conform to the ways parents in the dominant culture interact with the school and with their children at home. Schools can invite parents and community members to participate in the curriculum, thereby bringing their cultures into the school.

What Principals Can Do

Clearly, administrators are key to helping schools move towards becoming more responsive to diverse students and their families. Some of the specific actions principals can take include the following:

- Identify the needs and concerns of the community and become involved in helping it address the issues that are of importance to its members.
- Work continuously at expanding teachers' capacities to address the learning needs of children from culturally and linguistically diverse backgrounds, through appropriate staff development.
- Provide specific training for staff related to anti-racist and anti-bias teaching.
- Incorporate the enhancement of the school's multicultural practices as part of school improvement, and develop strategies for monitoring progress through gathering evidence.
- Devote resources to the development of language proficiency, making connections between the school and home lives of students.
- In setting high expectations for student learning in the school, ensure that the potential of students from culturally and linguistically diverse backgrounds is not underestimated because of language barriers. Set reasonable and attainable goals and monitor progress towards them.
- Review school policies to ensure that they set a framework for the inclusion of families from diverse ethnic, cultural, linguistic, and socioeconomic backgrounds.
- Personally invite parents and children from all cultures to participate in school activities.

- Ensure that the school provides rich learning environments that include multicultural and multilingual materials.
- Include parents and caregivers in the decision-making process regarding the curriculum and choice of materials, such as library resources. Invite them to contribute artifacts, and to participate in classroom and school multicultural activities to the extent that they feel comfortable.

Monitoring Progress

Including the enhancement of multicultural practices as a goal within a school improvement plan makes this aspect of the school's work an integral part of the school's efforts to maximize student learning.

Principals might use a checklist, such as the example provided in reproducible form on page 54, as a means of reflecting on the school's progress toward the goal. Principals can invite teachers and parents to provide input in response to the same questions.

It is particularly challenging for schools to support students whose home language is different from the language of instruction. Principals and teachers might find it helpful to use a questionnaire such as the one provided in reproducible form on page 55 (adapted from guidelines developed by Adams and Ferguson), in order to plan and monitor programs for second language learners.

Self-Assessment Checklist: How Multicultural is Our School?

School Culture and Climate

❏ Does our school demonstrate care and respect for all learners through its policies and practices?

❏ Does the physical environment visibly demonstrate, support, and celebrate our diverse communities (representation of diverse groups in displays, bulletin boards, and communications; signage in multiple languages; accommodation for cultural practices)?

❏ Is our school taking action to foster understanding and acceptance of cultural differences?

❏ Does our school invite the participation of diverse cultural groups and value the perspectives that they bring?

❏ Do all staff members — administrators, teachers, and support staff — demonstrate positive and respectful attitudes towards members of our diverse communities?

❏ Does the staff include members of diverse cultural and linguistic backgrounds?

Support for Students

❏ Does our school give priority to addressing the language-learning needs of students from diverse linguistic backgrounds?

❏ Does our school ensure that all students have equal access to high-quality programs?

❏ Do our assessment practices provide accommodation for students with linguistically and culturally diverse backgrounds, so that we are able to accurately monitor progress?

❏ Does our school have high expectations for all learners, whatever their diverse learning needs?

Curriculum and Instruction

❏ Do classroom resources and learning experiences represent the histories, experiences, and contributions of various cultural groups accurately and sensitively?

❏ Does our school draw upon students' family, language, and culture to enhance classroom learning?

❏ Do we create classroom environments in which we encourage and value different ways of learning and demonstrating learning?

Support for Staff

❏ Does our professional development give focus on learning about different cultural groups and how to work with diverse students and communities?

❏ Has our staff, both teachers and those in support roles, participated in professional development related to anti-racist and anti-bias practices?

❏ Does professional development include specific attention to assessing the learning of students with diverse linguistic and cultural backgrounds?

Relations with Parents and Community

❏ Does our school give priority to learning about its diverse communities?

❏ Does our school have in place supports that assist in two-way communication with parents from diverse linguistic backgrounds (translation services, staff members or volunteers who speak and write families' home languages, resources in multiple languages)?

❏ Does our school draw upon family and community resources across diverse communities to enhance learning?

❏ Does our school provide a variety of ways in which parents and community members can become involved?

❏ Does our school ensure that parents from diverse cultural and linguistic communities are able to participate in ongoing parent education and training, so parents can learn ways to enhance their child's learning at home?

Supporting Second Language Learners: Questions for Teachers to Consider

Program Planning

1. What do I already know about the second-language learners in my classroom and what other information do I need? What assessment techniques can I use to gather that information?
2. Drawing on the assessment information I have gathered, what specific language-learning experiences do each of my second-language learners need, based upon what I know about their language development?
3. How can demonstrate my respect for and understanding of my English for Speakers of Other Languages (ESOL) students' academic and linguistic backgrounds?
4. In what ways do individual ESOL learners need to adapt in order to become more successful in their new learning context; for example, to become accustomed to classroom structures and approaches to learning and assessment?

Cultural Respect and Sensitivity

1. In what ways may the cultural values of my ESOL students conflict with those of the dominant cultural context? How can I work proactively to avoid misunderstandings?
2. In what ways can I ensure that my classroom environment and learning experiences reflect the multiple cultures of the students?
3. How can I ease the transition of second-language learners, and provide social and emotional support?
4. How can I tailor the pace, sequence, and nature of language-learning experiences in relation to students' individual learning styles?

Language-rich Context

1. What language structures and vocabulary do my language learners already know?
2. What structures and words are likely to be unfamiliar?
3. How can I help students to feel confident and comfortable in participating? How can I avoid making them feel different or on the spot as they learn to use language in context?
4. How can I support learners through the use of visual, hands-on, or sensory experiences that help them develop understandings of content and make concrete connections with new concepts?

Time and Support to Develop Fluency

1. How can I ensure that each second-language learner has the support and time needed in order to become successful academically, given that the level of linguistic fluency needed to understand complex concepts is much greater than that needed in social settings?
2. In what ways can my second-language learners and I demonstrate to parents and other teachers that their language skills are developing, even though progress may seem slow?

CHAPTER 4 Gender and Schooling

Carefully observing and interacting with both girls and boys, principals and teachers can structure learning environments that are responsive to their varied needs and interests. Through such respectful attention to differences among learners, principals truly can make a difference.

Taking up the issues of gender and schooling these days is a bit like tiptoeing through a minefield. Reports of failing boys suggest that schools are now privileging girls at the expense of boys. Blame is heaped on feminists and female teachers for the feminization of schools. Although girls are doing better in science and math, the representation of women in careers in science and technology is still small. Despite changing societal values and norms, beliefs about what is appropriate for males and females evolve slowly. There is no doubt that schools reflect and perpetuate the values and attitudes of the sociocultural context in which they are situated; yet they also have a powerful influence over the future citizens of the communities they serve. As school and community leaders, principals are ideally positioned to challenge gender stereotypes that limit possibilities for both boys and girls.

Resisting deficit models that construct boys as "problem readers" or girls as somehow biologically unfit to be successful in math, science, and technology, schools under the leadership of informed principals can choose to focus on mobilizing the diverse strengths of the range of learners in their care. They can thoughtfully draw upon the insights of the research regarding the learning of boys and girls, recognizing that generalizations do not necessarily apply to *all* girls or *all* boys in *all* situations.

Analyzing the Achievement Gap

There is substantial evidence that girls are achieving at a higher level than boys, especially in the area of literacy, both reading and writing. Results of large-scale assessments internationally reflect this gender gap, and educational research in Canada, the United States, Australia, and Great Britain documents concerns regarding boys' attitudes and achievement. Many boys have negative views of school, don't like to read, and don't read well. In some countries, more boys are failing and fewer go on to post-secondary education (Blair & Sanford).

Some critics of feminism cite this as evidence that the proactive work of feminists to address the historic disadvantaging of girls through improving their education has now disadvantaged males. Claims that low achievement among boys is due to too much attention paid to girls or to the lack of male teachers in the elementary schools and the resulting feminization of children's early education oversimplify the complexities of gender and schooling. I believe that administrative and teaching staffs across the levels of public education should be representative of all the diverse groups that make up our society, and thus I have no argument against increasing the number of men in elementary schools. That notwithstanding, it seems that blaming female teachers for the issues around boys' academic performance only leads to polarization and the development of gender camps. Moreover, suggesting that boys are now intentionally being disadvantaged because girls are doing better takes us backwards in efforts to create gender equity.

Many feminist researchers (e.g., Epstein, Elwood, Hey & Maw) raise questions about focusing on academic achievement and testing as measures of success, and point to the continuing male dominance in the job market and income. There is strong evidence that sociocultural factors, such as race and social class, have as much influence on underachievement as gender. It's important to ask, "Which boys?" British researchers Myhill and Jones document how underachievement is as big an issue for ethnic minority groups and working-class white girls as it is for boys, and so we also need to ask, "Which girls?"

Despite the achievement gap between girls and boys, in the world of work, especially in the highest paying jobs, middle- and upper-class white males still maintain their dominance. As reporter Tim Hames wrote in the *London Times* on August 18, 2000,

> The world has not turned on its head, let alone traversed full circle. Anyone out there who thinks that, because boys have achieved only 46% of the all the A grades at A levels in August 2000, men will command only 46% of the most senior and lucrative posts available when this same group of teenagers hit their mid-30s, is either utterly crackers or has privately devised a means of rendering pregnancy, as it has been understood for the last four million years, entirely redundant.... The underlying dilemma in the British Education system is now, as it has been of a hundred years, if not more, still social class, not gender.

Although the boys are not doing as well as girls with school literacies, Blair and Sanford speculate,

> The abilities to navigate the Internet, experiment with alternative literacies and 'read' multiple texts simultaneously — morphing their own literacy practices to take up new literacies — will be perhaps more useful workplace skills than the ability to analyze a work of fiction or to write a narrative account. (p. 459)

Further, as Myhill and Jones showed in their research related to teacher and pupil perspectives of gender and achievement, "underachieving girls appeared to be almost invisible" (p. 20).

Researchers also raise questions about the tools that are used to assess literacy achievement. For example, does the focus on narrative reading and writing in many assessments privilege girls? Examining this research, Smith and Wilhelm note,

> The evidence of boys' relative lack of literacy skills and their continuing loss of ground is consistent across studies and forceful in its accumulated detail. But we worry that the arguments based on this data take for granted that the very tests that document the gaps are not gender-biased, a questionable assumption. (p. 3)

So, what sense can principals and teachers make of the evidence regarding the achievement of boys and girls? Macro-trends documented through large-scale assessments and employment statistics certainly yield important information. They are not very helpful, however, in pointing directions for practice. Research that has a focus on developing insights into how both boys and girls learn is much more useful and applicable.

I define gender equity as as creating conditions in which both girls and boys learn in appropriate, supportive educational contexts.

Blair and Sanford provide a summary of their ongoing research and suggestions for other resources at http://www.education.ualberta.ca/boysandliteracy/findings.html

Insights from Research

When considering research on gender and schooling, it's important to be clear on how gender is being defined. While there is no question that being male or female is biological, gender identities are largely socially constructed. The varied social and cultural contexts in which children live and learn provide different possibilities for being male or female. Images of men and women in popular culture both reflect and help construct gender identities. Gender possibilities change over time through the influence of social movements, such as feminist efforts to improve the education of girls and to expand the roles open for women. More recently, pro-feminist male researchers (e.g., Lingard & Douglas) have begun to argue that the range of possibilities for boys, too, needs to broaden through challenging dominant — and often stereotypical — versions of what it means to be male. Such researchers contend that the equity project taken up by feminists on behalf of girls needs to extend to boys, as well.

Learning from Neuroscience

Although I draw primarily upon a social constructivist perspective on gender and schooling, I think it is important to also be open to the insights that are emerging from neuroscience.

New technologies are providing more extensive information about the structure and function of the brain, demonstrating that there are gender differences in the way that the brain operates. The implications of these new insights for education are just being explored, but they do seem to have some explanatory power relating to the way girls and boys go about learning. Writing for an audience of educators, Gurian and Stevens provide a summary of the recent findings, with the caveat that these generalizations do not apply to all girls or all boys, that there are individual differences among boys and among girls in all aspects of brain structure and function.

In general, the following characterize the brains of girls.

- A larger corpus callosum (connecting tissue between hemispheres) enables more communication across hemispheres.
- Stronger neural connectors in temporal lobes lead to "more sensually detailed memory storage, better listening skills, and better discrimination among various tones of voice" (p. 22).
- A larger hippocampus enhances memory.
- A more active and earlier developed prefontal cortex and more serotonin lead to less impulsivity.
- There is more use of cortical areas for verbal and emotive functioning.

In contrast, boys' brains, in general

- use more cortical area for spatial-mechancial functioning
- have less serotonin and ocytocin (human bonding chemical), leading to greater impulsivity and less likelihood of overcoming this tendency through social relations
- are more lateralized in activity, so boys have more difficulty multi-tasking.
- renew and recharge through entering a rest state, leading to a greater tendency for boys to tune out, especially in contexts in which words rather than actions dominate.

Using more girl-friendly approaches, such as incorporating more verbal explanations, is positively affecting girls' achievement; however, as discussed earlier in this chapter, the long-term outcomes in terms of girls' future life prospects are changing more slowly.

This research suggests that girls have some biological advantages when learning literacy as it is currently taught in most schools where the emphasis is on verbal processing. As well, girls are more successful in traditional classrooms because of their greater capacity to sustain attention. Despite their relative disadvantage in spatial-mathematical functioning, there is evidence that girls are doing better in math and science because of efforts to address girls' education over the past several decades. Drawing on the insights regarding brain structure and function, Gurian and Stevens contend that similar adjustments need to be made for boys, by building "nature-based" classrooms. These practices include using concrete models and examples to support linguistic development, building in opportunities for movement and active involvement through experiential learning, using male role models and mentors, and teaching boys how to access and express emotions and feelings in socially appropriate ways.

Boys' Literacy Learning

A body of qualitative research describes what literacy learning is like for boys, offering some generalizations regarding the problems that many boys experience. Rather than working from a deficit model that positions boys as a problem, however, much of this research examines the strengths that boys bring to literacy learning and documents a mismatch between those strengths and many current classroom practices in literacy teaching and learning.

> With the caveat that these characteristics do not apply to all boys in all situations, the research shows that boys
>
> - generally learn to read more slowly than girls, read less, and are less enthusiastic about reading.
> - place a lower value on reading and writing than girls; they read less for pleasure and are more likely to choose informational texts.
> - are more likely to choose magazines, newspapers, comic books, and graphic novels.
> - like to read about things that they might like doing (sports, hobbies, how-tos).
> - tend to be more interested in reading associated with technology.
> - resist literacy because, as gender is constructed in some social and cultural contexts, it is seen as a female activity and not "manly."

Although these insights are of interest, I share the concern expressed by Smith and Wilhelm about the assumptions underlying many of the studies. First, the research oversimplifies and essentializes the complexities of literacy learning, assuming that gender is of significance and failing to take into consideration the differential impact of varied contexts and tasks on the learning of both boys and girls. Second, the research makes comparisons among groups or categories, thus losing the differences across individuals. Third, assessment of literacy performance is based on school tasks, rather than encompassing literacy practices outside of school, which often are much richer and more powerful.

Several more recent qualitative studies provide insights into the richness and variation in boys' literacy learning. Smith and Wilhelm's own study of a diverse group of adolescent boys shows that, across all categories of diversity, there were

The evidence cited in the study by Smith and Wilhelm demonstrates over and over that these young men were engaged with literacy. The problem seemed to be the mismatch between their literacy practices and preferences and the school literacy curriculum.

some characteristics that dominated. Above all, the boys wanted to have a sense of competence and control. For them all, literacy learning was inherently social. Many of the boys were deeply engaged in using a wide array of literacy practices outside school. For many, varied and sophisticated applications of technology facilitated social interaction. In terms of texts, the boys expressed preferences for

- stories rather than textbooks
- visual texts
- texts that could be brought into conversations
- texts, such as serials, that sustain engagement
- texts with multiple perspectives
- texts that bring surprise or novelty, are edgy or subversive, and contain powerful ideas or humor

A study by Blair and Sanford of somewhat younger boys documents how boys "morph" school tasks, transforming them into literacy practices more suited to their interests and ways of learning. The researchers observed, "They do this in many ways: by using characters from their out of school literacies to match their interests, by livening up the activity, by changing and converting the teacher's instructions, or by including elements of humor and satire in their reading and writing" (p. 453). Many of the boys were struggling with school literacies, but they demonstrated rich literacy engagement outside of school with media texts, computer games, sports magazines, comics, and other graphic texts. In school they preferred fantasy, action stories, and information texts with "action and violence, games/competition, challenges, and satire" (p. 456). Some of the boys did not seem to function well within the classroom structure, needing a more flexible and supportive environment in which there were larger time frames to complete tasks. In many classrooms, teachers did not acknowledge and value the boys' out-of-school literacy competencies, and thus the boys struggled to make connections with the school curriculum.

In order to engage boys in literacy, schools need to meet them where they are, drawing on the genres that they enjoy to help them grow.

In another study of young boys' literacy, Newkirk makes a strong case that the devaluing of boys' preferences does them a significant disservice. Schools set up a hierarchy of "good" and "not good" texts, discounting such narrative forms as television, video games, and comic books. Further, schools misread boys' fascination with violence in their reading and writing, sending up signals of alarm rather than attempting to understand how both boys and girls draw upon popular culture and other narrative forms as they develop as literacy users. He offers an alternative explanation for the violence, showing how boys use their reading and writing to role-play, exercising control and power in fictional worlds. Boys also use action-oriented literacy practices to make social connections. He suggests that teachers and parents need to work with children, emphasizing the development of plausible story lines and the use of suspense and action rather than gratuitous violence. Adults also need to be attuned to the way boys, in particular, take pleasure from crude forms of humor, both as readers and writers.

Researcher and parent Bronwyn Williams writes eloquently about her conflicts over her own son's violent writing. Recognizing his power as a writer, she nevertheless cringes at the violence depicted in many of his stories and reflects thoughtfully about how parents and teachers should respond. She notes that, as an adult reader, she enjoys action and suspense. She wonders, if she can get pleasure from these texts and keep the separation between fiction and real life, why can't we also trust boys to make that distinction? Why do we assume that violence expressed in literacy practices necessarily translates into violent actions? At the conclusion of her article, Williams raises provocative questions (p. 514) that all educators need to consider as they work with both boys and girls.

- What do we want young people to learn about literacy?
- Is character analysis necessarily the pinnacle of literacy practice?
- If we say we are trying to teach creative and critical thinking through literacy, what activities do we imagine will achieve this, and what will such literacy look like?
- Are our students engaging in literacy practices outside the classroom that we should pay more attention to and work with rather than against?
- Do we need to reconsider what creative literacy practices and thoughtful and analytical literacy look like?
- What choices, options, and possibilities can we offer?
- Most important, how can we help boys and girls learn about the many different ways that reading and writing can provide them with power, choice, and flexibility as they become adults?

The questions that Williams poses seem to me to be a helpful tool for thinking through how best to support both boys and girls as literacy learners. They might make an interesting beginning point for a principal's discussions with staff about the assumptions underlying a school's literacy program.

Girls, Science, Math, and Technology

As I noted earlier, despite the higher participation and greater success of girls in science, math, and technology courses in school, they continue to be significantly under-represented in the careers in science, engineering, and technology. A study by the Nova Scotia Advisory Council on the Status of Women (2004) showed that, in 2001, women continued to be over-represented by large percentages in the ten lowest-paid occupations in the province, primarily in the service industries. Women are also significantly under-represented in the ten highest-paid occupations, largely professional and managerial positions. Statistics Canada data on employment trends in 2001 showed women and men were almost equally represented in the employed labour force, but the percentage of women's representation in science, technology, and trades was, in most areas, in the single digits. In Nova Scotia the employment of women in computer and information system occupations (professional) actually decreased from 36.6% in 1991 to 25.5% in 2001. The percentage of women in trades remained constant at less than 5%.

With the current significant shortage of skilled workers in a variety of trades expected to become even more of a problem as Baby Boomers retire, girls need to have equal access to these careers. As reported in the Toronto *Globe and Mail* in January 2005, "Where plumbers and pipe fitters may once have struggled with meagre pay and even less respect, they are now commanding wages for their work that are thousands of dollars more than university graduates with desk jobs and a framed arts degree on the wall." Elementary school is not too early to begin to develop girls' abilities and confidence in engaging in activities that historically have been considered boyish.

A review of the research related to girls' career choices (Manicom, Armour, Sewell, & Parsons) identified five factors that influence girls' educational and career choices:

Five factors that influence girls' educational and career choices:

- attitudes and expectations of parents and teachers
- learning environments, teaching strategies, and instructional materials
- images of science and technology
- science and technology workplaces
- self-concept and sense of a "future self"

- **The attitudes and expectations of parents and teachers:** As mentioned in the previous chapter, both parents and teachers can either limit or expand the possibilities for children of both genders through the role models they provide and through their attitudes. Stereotypes about girls' inability to analyze or deal with the technical can become self-fulfilling prophecies, just as beliefs about boys not liking to read limit literacy development.

- **Learning environments, teaching strategies, and instructional materials:** All aspects of girls' school experiences should open possibilities for them to be successful in math, science, and technology. Resources need to reflect the accomplishments of women, and girls need to see women teachers in math, science, and technology classrooms. Approaches to instruction need to build upon girls' strengths in verbal thinking and involve them in meaningful investigation rather than rote learning. Recent research shows that girls have more equal access to computers in school than in the past, but the instructional practices often do not engage them. They find programming classes dull and many computer games boring, useless, and too violent.

Although schools cannot change the workplace conditions that students will face when they leave school, both teachers and administrators can have an impact on four of the five factors that influence girls' career decisions.

- **Images of science and technology:** Research shows that girls see careers in science and technology as "objective, rational, hard, elitist, overly competitive, and lacking in a human dimension" (Manicom et al, p. 9). Girls' beliefs about the trades are even more negative. These stereotypes do not reflect the way that science and technology are actually carried out, where creative and relational thinking are as necessary as more rational and analytical thought. The dominance of men in the field limits the ability of women to have an impact on how technology evolves, as Margolis and Fisher note:

While girls and women may be using the Internet for communication and the web for information retrieval, it is predominantly men who are programming the computers, designing and fixing the systems, and inventing the technology that will affect all aspects of our lives. The under-representation of women among the creators of technology has serious consequences, not only for those women who potential goes unrealized, but also for a society increasingly shaped by that technology.

- **Science and technology workplaces:** Although there is a theoretical acknowledgment that women bring many strengths to the fields of science and technology, the actual workplaces are slow to respond to the diversity that greater representation of women brings. The need for women to combine work and home responsibilities to a far greater extent than men and to interrupt employment because of pregnancy still influence women's career choices and trajectories.

- **Self-concept and sense of a "future self":** Studies continue to show that girls believe that they are less capable than boys in science and math. Further, girls take into consideration issues such as the nature of the work (whether it involves working with other people or alone) and the need to balance family and work responsibilities. The girls' beliefs that careers in science, technology, and trades are not appropriate future directions for them may, given the current scarcity of family-friendly workplaces, be based on a realistic assessment of the world of work. Such beliefs, however, continue to limit the possibilities for girls to pursue many rewarding career possibilities in the knowledge society.

Implications for School and Classroom

Along with other researchers who view the issues of gender and schooling from a social constructivist perspective, I am hopeful regarding the possibilities for changing outcomes for both boys and girls through classroom practices informed by the messages of research.

Beliefs, attitudes, and behaviors that limit possibilities for both genders derive from stereotypical notions of what it means to be a man or a woman. Schools have the responsibility, not only to contest those stereotypes, but also to respond to the strengths and interests that boys and girls bring to the classroom. This means moving past the issue of "problem boys" to raising expectations and to developing a more responsive curriculum. It means helping girls see themselves as future mathematicians, engineers, scientists, technologists, and practitioners of historically male-dominated trades. It means listening to both boys and girls, observing them closely, and identifying their needs. Outlined below are some specific suggestions for school and classrooms practices.

Develop Supportive Cultures for Learning

If both girls and boys are to learn to their potential, school and classroom cultures need to support their full participation in learning. Principals and teachers help to create such cultures when they

- use gender-neutral language.
- challenge sexist language and behaviors.
- look beyond gender stereotypes to recognize and develop the individual strengths of students.
- ensure that the school and classroom environments (posters, bulletin boards, and other visuals) reflect diverse groups in a variety of learning situations and roles.
- sensitize students to biased materials, encouraging them to critique and challenge instances of bias that they discover.
- explore stereotypes when reading or in general discussion; for example, asking if characters in books or on television are realistic portrayals or if they perpetuate stereotypes.
- encourage a cooperative and accepting environment in which it is safe to express ideas and opinions
- use small cooperative groups and encourage the active participation of all, especially less assertive students of both genders.

- incorporate a variety of ways to manage student responses: for example, putting students' name in a hat and drawing from it; numbering students and calling out numbers until all have participated; using a talking stick that gives a speaker the floor until finished, with no interruptions from more vocal students; assigning roles within small groups so that each person has the chance to be spokesperson.

Proactively Address Issues of Harassment

Sexual harassment, both verbal and physical, continues to affect both boys and girls in school, despite the widespread institution of sexual harassment policies in schools over the past decade. Although boys and girls are almost equally subject to sexual harassment, girls' education is more likely to be negatively affected because they seem to take it more to heart, losing confidence and developing negative self-esteem.

Research on bullying and sexual harassment, and a downloadable guide to Harassment Free Hallways, can be accessed at the AAUW web site: www.aauw.org

> The research, such as a 2001 report of the American Association of University Women (AAUW), shows that sexual harassment is part of everyday life in school, beginning at the elementary level. Forms of sexual harassment reported by students include making sexual comments, jokes, gestures, or looks; spreading sexual rumors; calling others gay or lesbian; unwanted touching, grabbing, or contact; and making someone very uncomfortable.

Through educative rather than punitive approaches, schools can do a great deal to prevent harassment:

1. Create clear policies that are easy to understand and disseminate widely (post in the school, include in student handbook, distribute to parents). Some schools also create pamphlets designed to be appealing to students, showing what sexual harassment is and how the school's policy protects them.
2. Once the policy has been developed, involve staff, students, and parents in workshops related to the policy.
3. Provide additional training for staff, students, and parents in how to recognize and respond to sexual harassment, as well as how to prevent its occurrence.
4. Designate sexual harassment contact persons in the school, at least one male and one female. These individuals provide a safe person to whom victims can go and report incidents. The contact persons should receive additional training related to all aspects of sexual harassment.
5. Involve students actively as leaders of peer education related to sexual harassment, discussing the importance of taking action rather than standing by when someone is being harassed.
6. Form partnerships with community agencies that the school can draw upon for counseling and victim support.
7. Incorporate attention to issues of sexual harassment within the curriculum. Case studies are an excellent tool for raising issues and exploring solutions.
8. Set good examples for students through avoiding sexual references, jokes, and innuendo.

Expand the Literacy Curriculum

Definitions of literacy are expanding to include visual, electronic, and media forms, along with print. Literacy research has given a focus to the strengths and interests boys demonstrate in their use of these forms of literacy outside school; however, it is equally important that the curriculum for girls reflect "real world" forms of literacy. Invite both boys and girls to bring out-of-school literacy texts and practices into the classroom, and include these sources on an equal basis with literary and informational texts and more "schoolish" literacy practices. Some specific suggestions:

- Provide a range of opportunities for students to read, write, and represent in multiple forms.
- Draw on pop culture, such as magazines, music, television, videos, films, and electronic texts. Learn about these texts from the students.
- Encourage students to use pop culture forms in their writing and representation.

Incorporate Boy-friendly Approaches to Literacy Learning

Because of concerns about boys' literacy achievement, the focus of both researchers and practitioners has been developing a better understanding of their needs and interests.

1. Include more humor in texts and classroom activities. Create spaces for boys — especially those at elementary age — to express the crude forms of humor they enjoy so much. Draw on comics and humorous television shows to teach narrative structures and literary conventions. Make cartooning a serious business to tap into many boys' fascination with the art form.
2. When making instructional decisions about texts for boys in both reading and writing contexts, take the following into consideration.

   - Length: For boys who are reluctant to read, long texts present a huge, sometimes insurmountable, challenge. Build a collection of short and interesting texts. Invite boys to experiment with short pieces of writing, emulating forms that they enjoy as readers: for example, they might write narratives based on computer game stories.
   - Choice: Provide more options for students and work with them to help them make wise choices. This not only allows them to express their interests and preferences, but contributes to feelings of control that are important for boys. Myhill and Jones cite research that shows that boys perform extremely well in writing when given the opportunity to write about subjects of their own choice.
   - Genre: Although engagement with literary texts is important, ensure that boys have access to a wide variety of informational texts, and encourage them to develop power and authority as writers in expository modes. To enhance boys' confidence and capabilities in dealing with literary texts, give emphasis to action stories, science fiction, crime fiction, sports stories, and other literature with boy appeal.

3. As much as possible, make reading and writing social. Smith and Wilhelm advocate "group structures such as literary letter exchanges, book clubs, literature circles, cooperative learning groups, reading buddies, reciprocal reading groups" (p. 199). Encourage the use of talk for learning, and incorporate drama.

A web site that includes a section on gender and literacy and provides links to many other resources and research reports is www.literacytrust.org.uk

While the following suggestions draw on the messages of the research related to boys, many of them apply equally to some or all girls.

When working with young male writers, Newkirk suggests that teachers need to accept and celebrate youth genres, which have the following characteristics: fiction is a way for young boys, in particular, to take on competencies and power that they don't possess in real life, a form of "wish fulfillment"; narratives are quickly paced, with emphasis on action; writing affirms friendship groups, often featuring characters with names of people in the writer's social group; the writing is often silly, even slapstick, with crude forms of humor and sound effects.

4. Build curriculum around active problem solving and inquiry. Encourage students to identify questions they wish to explore and then build literacy experiences around their inquiry into those questions. Such an approach enhances interest and engagement, but also provides the flexibility in the use of time that Blair and Sanford's research has shown is important to boys' success. Further, boys can see real purposes for their reading and writing, and can develop a sense of competence in relation to the questions/topics they explore.

5. Use less teacher talk and incorporate demonstrations, visuals, and activities that get students moving, talking, and thinking.

6. Emphasize purpose and application. When working with boys, make sure they can answer the question, "What will I use this for?"

7. Teach students how to read different kinds of texts, providing what Smith and Wilhelm call "frontloading." Given the importance to boys of feeling competent and having an appropriate level of challenge, such instruction helps boys gain insights into how different texts work. With that prior knowledge, they are more likely to tackle new and challenging material.

Encourage the Participation of Girls in Math, Science, and Technology

While these suggestions derive from research related to girls, they represent sound practices for many boys as well.

Reflecting on the implications of recent brain research discussed earlier, Gurian and Stevens (p. 73) suggest the following ways elementary classrooms can become more supportive to girls' education:

- Play physical games to promote gross motor skills. Girls are behind boys in this area when they start school.
- Have portable/digital cameras around and take pictures of girls being successful at tasks.
- Use water and sand tables to promote science in a spatial venue.
- Use lots of puzzles to foster perceptual learning.
- Form working groups and teams to promote leadership roles and negotiation skills.
- Use manipulatives to teach math.
- Verbally encourage the hidden high energy of the quieter girls.

While suggestions for science and technology classrooms are designed for secondary schools, all of them could be adapted for younger students.

Manicom et al offer the following specific suggestions (p. 41) for science and technology classrooms:

- Discuss the image of science and technology.
- Help students become informed of the issues for females in science and technology.
- If necessary, supplement the text with examples of women scientists and technologists and provide examples of women in other non-stereotypical roles.
- Discuss the accomplishments of women scientists and technologists and have students research their contributions.
- Relate science and technology to everyday life experiences of females as well as males, and stress social applications of science and technology in everyday life.
- Design activities that are supportive of female-friendly learning and require students to use logical reasoning; plan investigations; create drawings, graphs, tables, and charts; hypothesize about expected outcomes; draw on their own experience; give more than one answer; be creative when conducting investigations.

What Principals Can Do

Lesley Traves, a head teacher in England, achieved dramatic improvements in the performance of boys on national assessments of reading by changing the school's reading culture.

In their roles as school leaders, principals can have a significant impact on the learning of both boys and girls by applying what we know about gender and schooling.

Set Clear Expectations

Work with staff to develop positive attitudes and behaviors in relation to the education of both boys and girls. Lead by example by instituting principles of equity in dealing with all students and ensuring that all boys and girls are full participants in all aspects of the curriculum.

Staff Development

Focus staff development on issues related to gender and learning. Gather evidence on the achievement of girls and boys across the grades in school, using available test results and classroom assessments. Share highlights of the research relating to boys and literacy, and relating to girls and science and technology; invite staff to consider its relevance in the particular school context.

Contest Gender Stereotypes

A study of teacher and pupil perspectives of gender and achievement through the University of Exeter in England (Myhill & Jones) revealed that even teachers who espoused principles of equity and said that they avoided gender stereotyping in their teaching reflected those stereotypes in their attitudes when interviewed. The researchers reported,

> When talking about boys and girls, in general, teachers portrayed boys far more negatively than girls and described boys as lazy, disruptive, aggressive, with poor concentration and less likely to take education seriously. Girls, on the other hand, want to please, apply themselves, are quieter and efficient and are more enthusiastic. (p. 20)

When boys did achieve well, the teachers considered it an anomaly. Underachieving girls tended to be overlooked, and some of the teachers mentioned that they were more likely to be compliant and quiet, and so could easily be missed. The children, too, regardless of gender, thought that girls were smarter and more likely to succeed. As a school leader, the principal can work with teachers and students to contest such stereotypes. As a first step, invite teachers to examine their attitudes and beliefs about student achievement through such questions as

- How do we as individuals and as school as a whole identify students who are underachieving?
- How do we know if students are achieving to their potential? What factors do we take into consideration? Do we look at boys and girls differently?
- How are we supporting both boys and girls who are not working to their potential?
- What strengths do individual boys and girls bring to literacy learning?

Make Classrooms More Boy- and Girl-friendly

Enhance teachers' knowledge of boy- and girl-friendly pedagogies. Using the implications for practice outlined above as a starting point, challenge teachers to make their classrooms more friendly to both boys and girls.

Give Specific Attention to Boys and Literacy

The web site at www.guysread.com is a good starting place for suggested titles of books boys like to read.

While keeping in mind the individual differences among boys and girls, principals can help boys who are underachieving in literacy through the following types of interventions.

- Build relationships with boys, demonstrating that they are valued and liked. Make a point to notice their accomplishments and to give positive feedback, assuring them that they are part of the literate culture of the school whether they read novels or comic books.
- Devote as much funding as possible to expanding school and classroom library collections to include boy-friendly texts. Ask boys to help in building these collections by identifying topics and genres of interest to them. Invite boys to bring out-of-school literacy texts into the classroom/ school.
- Build the school's capacities in the use of technology to support learning. Work to acquire hardware and develop staff expertise in the use of a range of technologies. Provide opportunities for boys and girls to demonstrate leadership and to bring their out-of-school literacy practices into the school.
- Involve parents and caregivers and support their efforts. Traves recounts how important parents were in changing boys' attitudes towards reading. The school shared the evidence it had collected regarding boys' achievement and then challenged parents, especially fathers and other male caregivers, to become part of the solution by helping boys read and providing role models. The school provided lots of support through easily accessible pamphlets on tips for helping, workshops, and book sales.
- Provide male role models within the school. Some schools have trained fathers to run study skills sessions and to read with students in the school. This could be a focus for recruitment of school volunteers.
- Celebrate boys' literacy practices. Provide opportunities for boys to demonstrate their strengths with out-of-school literacies; for example, having them contribute to the school's web site, publish their electronic and graphic texts, and share their stories in pop culture forms.

Make the Inclusion of Girls in Science, Math, and Technology a Priority

Although there is evidence that both the participation rates and success of girls in math, science, and technology has improved over the past several decades, this has not translated into the broadening of females' career choices and options. Principals can address this continuing problem by giving priority to the following:

- Help parents develop a better understanding of issues for girls in science and technology. Invite their participation in changing stereotypical beliefs and attitudes.
- Provide female role models by making female teachers visible in mathematics, science, and technology in the classroom. Draw on resources

in the community, inviting women engaged in science, technology, and trades to participate in volunteer programs in the school and to serve as mentors to girls.

- Help girls become more technologically savvy.

A report by the AAUW, *Educating Girls in the New Computer Age*, has a number of recommendations that principals can act upon.

- Shift emphasis from access to computers to computer fluency: i.e., girls' mastery of analytical skills, computer concepts, and capacity for imaginative applications of technology to solve a range of problems.
- Choose software based upon its potential to engage a wide variety of learners, not just the "geeks" who already are hooked on technology.
- Invite girls to use their imaginations, tinkering with the technology in creative ways so that they can see themselves as designers as well as users.
- Infuse technology concepts and uses across the curriculum, and in such areas as the arts, to capture the interests of girls and increase the likelihood that they will see themselves as future leaders in the high-tech economy and culture.
- Provide professional development to help teachers move beyond using computers as productivity tools and understand the power of technology in learning and creative problem solving.
- Contest the stereotypical images that those who work with technology operate in isolation, and help girls understand the range of career possibilities that combine interactions with people and opportunities for creative and inventive thinking with technology.

Community groups and businesses may be interested in partnering around the development of activities that enhance girls' awareness of the possibilities for future education and work in the areas of science, technology, and trades.

- Make community connections through parents, service groups, women's groups, universities and colleges, businesses, cultural groups, or professional organizations. These can be sources of mentors for girls. Manicom et al found that high school girls were, for the most part, unaware of post-secondary education possibilities other than attending university, so making connections with community colleges, trade schools, and other specialized training institutions can open new possibilities. Young adolescent girls in late-elementary, middle, or junior-high school are already beginning to develop perceptions about their "future selves," so it is not too early to begin expanding their horizons and encouraging their interest in careers they might not have imagined for themselves.

CHAPTER 5   Making Sense of Accountability

In the late 1980s I attended a workshop led by Margaret Meek Spencer, an internationally respected British literacy researcher and educator, in which she posed the question, "What will be the dominant discourse of the 1990s?" The group guessed a number of possibilities, but did not come up with the answer that Margaret had in mind: accountancy. She predicted that public education systems would become obsessed with accounting for achievement, finances, and the efficient use of resources. Anyone who has lived through the never-ending series of reforms and improvement plans that have dominated life in public education over the past decade and a half knows that Margaret foretold the future very accurately.

There is no way that anyone currently working in public education can ignore the issue of accountability. Over the last several decades, large-scale external assessments have taken on ever-increasing importance as a means of judging the performance of schools and school districts. The realities of today's context demand that principals and teachers become as knowledgeable as they can about these tests and the appropriate use of the data they yield. Even more important, however, is becoming skilled at classroom assessment and in the use of school-based data that provides a rich and nuanced picture of student learning and of the school as a whole. The thoughtful use of such data enables schools to "speak for themselves" as British researcher MacBeath so aptly puts it. Taking responsibility for assessment in this way provides schools the opportunity to determine what counts as data, and to use that data to inform ongoing self-evaluation and learning.

As literacy researcher Peter Johnston has pointed out, being *responsible* implies a different relationship than being *accountable*. Teachers and administrators are responsible to and for their students and their families. They also have a responsibility to the larger system and wider community as employees of a publicly funded education system. Accountability suggests an outside-in relationship, in which others regulate educators and hold them accountable; responsibility comes from within. Responsibility carries with it a level of trust and professionalism that is absent when the focus is on accountability. As well, Johnston (1992) notes, "It is possible to be held accountable, but at the same time not to be responsible" (p. 6).

Accountability measures, such as large-scale external assessment, put the focus entirely on assessment *of* learning, in the past more commonly called "summative assessment." In contrast, classroom assessment gives emphasis to assessment *for* learning; that is, using information about students' learning to provide feedback to the learners themselves and to inform the teachers' instruction. This was at one time more frequently referred to as "formative assessment." A number of years ago Black and Wiliam conducted an extensive review of the research regarding

Across public sector institutions such as health, education, and social services, administrators must meet expectations for evidence-based decision making. School improvement efforts must be data-driven.

Summative assessment: assessment *of* learning
Formative assessment: assessment *for* learning, to provide feedback to learners and to inform teachers' instruction

the impact of different kinds of assessment on student achievement. They cited substantial evidence that improving assessment for learning (formative assessment) is the most powerful way to improve student learning, particularly if students themselves are active participants in the process. The research shows that increasing specific, descriptive feedback and decreasing evaluative feedback combine to bring about gains in student achievement. They concluded, "There is a body of firm evidence that formative assessment is an essential component of classroom work and that its development can raise standards of achievement. We know of no other way of raising standards for which such a strong prima facie case can be made" (p. 148).

Creating Coherence

See Chapter 6 for a discussion on how principals can strive for greater coherence in their schools.

In Laura's school, bringing a focus to student assessment proved to be a powerful means of drawing together multiple initiatives and of bringing a school-wide focus to student learning. When the district invited schools to participate in the pilot stage of a long-term assessment and evaluation initiative, Laura jumped at the chance to become involved.

> Laura envisioned her school's participation with other schools in developing an assessment policy for the district, and in generating a school plan for assessing and communicating student learning, as a way to connect the many different strands of her work in the school. She told me,
>
> > We'll get at our language arts and our math. Yes, absolutely. And I think that's what's going to happen. And right now schools that are into implementation of the new curriculum guides, most schools have picked one discipline: it's either language arts or math, and they have a plan, and it's done in chunks. With assessment, we will get at all of that. It won't just look like a curriculum implementation plan, but it's actually what we will be doing because we'll be looking at assessment in terms of the learning outcomes.... Even talking about how our school assemblies are a form of reporting to parents and what kind of language would you use to report to parents that, when a child is on the stage reciting a poem or telling a story, [it has] to do with learning outcomes?...The parents who don't understand why, in preparation of the concert in December, we have three weeks of rehearsals [think that] you're taking away from instructional time to do concert rehearsals. It's not only a hard sell with parents, it's sometimes a hard sell with teachers. Well, why do we do that and what has that got to do with a communication plan and communicating student learning? And what does it look like within the framework of the outcomes? And I'm delighted because to me it just solidifies everything.

Laura's personal reflections on the role of assessment in her school mirror the messages of the research summarized by Black and Wiliam. In the last decade there have been substantive efforts to translate that research into action within schools. Improving classroom assessment is a complex process of working with teachers over the long term to expand their knowledge about a range of assessment practices, including the appropriate use of information from large-scale external assessments, and to assist them in incorporating those practices in the classroom. Leaders of these efforts, such as Stiggins in the United States and Davies in Canada, emphasize the importance of providing high-quality and sustained professional development in order to support teachers in the difficult process of making complex changes in how they think and work. Investment in such efforts, according to Stiggins (2004), is the best means to reach school improvement goals since, "Achievement gains of the magnitude seen in the research on balanced assessment are unprecedented in the literature of school improvement" (p. 27).

Stiggins and other assessment leaders (Chappuis, Stiggins, Arter & Chappuis; Chappuis) argue that principals need to enhance their knowledge and skills in assessment for learning in order to lead change efforts in their schools. By so doing, school leaders are better positioned to use classroom assessment as a catalyst for improving student learning. Some ways principals provide such leadership:

- Working with teachers to establish shared expectations for student achievement, translating provincial or state standards and curricular frameworks into learning goals that are teachable and assessable.
- Giving a focus to expanding the range and quality of assessments teachers use in their classrooms.
- Involving students in the assessment process.
- Engaging teachers in professional growth processes related to improvement of classroom assessment as part of teacher evaluation.
- Monitoring the implementation of assessment practices
- Enhancing the quality of communication about student learning by helping parents understand learning expectations and by reporting student progress in relation to those expectations.

Classroom Assessment *for* and *of* Learning

It's clearly well beyond the scope of this book to provide a comprehensive discussion of classroom assessment. My purpose here is to provide a summary of key insights that may be helpful to principals as they think through how best to move forward in their schools. In undertaking something as complex as improving assessment practices to enhance student learning it is helpful, if not essential, to begin with a big picture of the undertaking. I offer the following as some of the important features to take into consideration when constructing that picture.

Principles and Frameworks

We all work from theories in our head about how the world works. These theories, often unarticulated, shape our practices as teachers and administrators. Becoming more explicit about the principles that underlie assessment practices provides a beginning place for teachers to reaffirm and revise what they believe and how they teach and assess. Drawing on current research, Stiggins (2001) identifies the following guiding principles:

- Students are the key assessment users.
- Clear and appropriate targets are essential.
- Accurate assessment is a must.
- Sound assessment must be accompanied by effective communication.

Davies' web site provides regularly updated information related to assessment, opportunities for professional development, and relevant print resources: http://www.connect2learning.com

Davies also gives emphasis to involving students, establishing and using criteria, setting goals, collecting evidence, and using that evidence in communicating. I prefer Davies' terminology: "criteria" and "goals" instead of "targets." While I recognize that the use of "target" emphasizes the need to be extremely clear and focused in regard to intentions and expectations for student learning, I find the word's association with weapons troubling. That notwithstanding, I take no issue with the underlying principle — it is essential to articulate achievement expectations in specific language that reflects the current best insights into what it means to be successful in a particular aspect of learning. That means being able to describe different levels of performance based upon criteria. For example, assessing students' responses to a writing assignment involves defining the attributes of a good piece of that genre of writing, and then determining how well each writer has performed in relation to those criteria.

Davies provides a helpful framework for thinking about the kinds of evidence that should be collected to maximize the information available on each student's learning. Through a process of triangulation, teachers collect and use three types of evidence: observations, conversations, and products. With a prior understanding of the goals and criteria of learning, both teachers and students use these multiple forms of evidence to determine how the learner is progressing. The evidence that is collected and used on an ongoing basis guides learners in knowing how they can move forward and in setting goals for future learning. Teachers use the evidence to make appropriate decisions regarding focused instruction and other learning experiences that will be most helpful to the learner. When it comes time to focus on assessment *of* learning — that is, to make comparisons with learning expectations or standards and to report on progress — teachers reflect upon and summarize the evidence. They need to be able to answer the question "Did the student learn what she or he needed to learn? How well?" (p. 41)

Student-involved Assessment

See page 81 for some suggestions for teacher professional development that take into consideration the complexities of making such significant changes in classrooms.

There are a number of ways students can become more fully engaged in classroom assessment. For many teachers, making the shifts in practice that result in students being the key users of assessment means a significant rethinking of roles and relationships in the classroom. Therefore, principals need to move slowly and supportively in working with teachers to incorporate any or all of the aspects of student-involved assessment summarized below. Student involvement might include

Participation in Setting and Using Criteria: Teachers can engage students in reviewing samples and models that exemplify different levels of performance on a particular aspect of learning. There can also be ongoing discussions with students about what constitutes success on different tasks and about the quality of their performance or response in relation to the criteria. Students can be involved in developing rubrics that describe levels of performance in terms of observable traits. This process requires the developers to agree upon language that is descriptive, specific, and understandable to all users. The negotiation that is required to achieve that end contributes to a deeper understanding of criteria for success.

Goal Setting: When students become more knowledgeable about criteria for learning, they are better able to set goals for their own learning in relation to those criteria. Such goal-setting increases students' self-direction and motivation.

Teacher–Student Conversations: Teachers help learners enhance their capacities for self-assessment through their interactions with students. Teachers can demonstrate how to give specific feedback through their comments and questions. As students gain experience, teachers can encourage the learners to take the lead in these conversations.

Davies (p. 7) suggests three categories of self-assessment activities:

- Pause and think: take a few minutes for reflection while learning
- Look for proof: select a work sample that demonstrates an aspect of learning and comment on it
- Connect to criteria: assess work in relation to established criteria and find evidence to demonstrate the level of performance

Self-Assessment: Teachers can support students' self-assessment by encouraging them to be reflective about their own learning. This involves students giving themselves descriptive feedback on their learning in relation to the agreed upon criteria and monitoring progress toward goals. This feedback can be informal and ongoing, but should be documented and shared through reflective journals or learning logs, checklists, or interactions with the teacher or peers.

Peer Assessment: When students provide feedback to each other through peer assessment, they gain further experiences in working with criteria. Learners also have the opportunity to take into consideration the views of others in relation to their learning.

Collection of Evidence: Students themselves can take responsibility for collecting different kinds of evidence of their learning. They can organize and share this evidence in different ways. Many teachers help students develop portfolios that include evidence of learning in a variety of forms, such as work samples, photographs, and artifacts. Students' reflections on why items are included and what each demonstrates about their learning are essential features of portfolios.

Presenting Evidence: Portfolios are one tool that teachers and students can use in communicating learning through the presentation of evidence. When students are involved in presenting evidence of their learning to an audience — whether the teacher, peers, students in another class, parents, or members of the community — it creates a context in which they must articulate what they know about their own achievement in ways that others will understand. As students respond to questions and comments, and receive feedback from others, they gain deeper insights into their learning.

Communicating Learning

When students are active participants in classroom assessment, communication about learning occurs on an ongoing basis. This day-to-day communication can expand to include regular interactions with parents through public displays of student work, teacher newsletters, sending home work samples, and informal interactions between teachers and parents regarding each child's accomplishments. Parents can be involved in goal setting with students and in helping them collect evidence of learning at home. Many schools have instituted student-led parent conferences in which students share their learning with parents. Students

It is helpful if teachers and students prepare a form that provides questions or prompts to guide feedback in student-led parent conferences; for example, asking the parent to notice something positive and to suggest an improvement.

Report cards usually include comments through which teachers can give feedback on what is going well and what learners can do to improve. Evaluative feedback can include coded symbols in the form of letter grades or numbers; words such as "excellent," "well done," or "needs improvement"; or checkmarks.

develop an agenda for these meetings and bring with them evidence of their learning (work samples, portfolios, projects). They may demonstrate an aspect of their learning; for example, they might read aloud a short text. The student leads the discussion of the evidence and then invites parents to give feedback. The sessions often conclude with goal-setting for future learning.

The more meaningfully teachers engage parents as participants in the assessment processes, the more likely it is that parents will support the efforts of the school to enhance student achievement. When it comes time to communicate more formally through whatever grading and reporting structures the school is required to use, parents will already be knowledgeable about their children's progress. Three-way student–parent–teacher conferences conducted at reporting time provide opportunities for all three to discuss evidence of learning and areas needing improvement. Written report cards become just one means of providing information to parents, not the sole form of communication. These forms of reporting provide a summary of the student's performance in a specific area of the curriculum or aspect of learning.

According to Davies (p. 67), when evaluating and reporting you must address four questions:

1. What does the student know and what is he or she able to do?
2. What areas require further attention or development?
3. In what ways can the students' learning be supported?
4. How is the student progressing in relation to the standards of development for students in a similar age range?

Answering these questions involves the teacher reviewing multiple forms of evidence (student self-assessments, teacher observations, assessments of assignments and projects based on criteria, rubrics used to assess performances, marks from tests), summarizing the insights gained through the review, and making comparisons with expectations or standards that describe learning. Inviting students and parents to have input into these evaluations provides information that improves their quality and validity.

Using Large-Scale Assessments

Despite the acknowledgment, even of those who create these tests, that large-scale assessment can provide only a limited range of information, the tests continue to be a highly publicized means of judging the effectiveness of teachers and schools.

Information on student achievement gathered through large-scale assessments, including both standardized tests and criterion-referenced assessments, garners the lion's share of media attention and government investment. Most of us are all too familiar with headlines that point out the successes and failures of schools and systems in relation to these assessments. There is compelling evidence that the tests have not contributed to significant improvements in student learning over a number of decades. Summarizing the messages of research, Stiggins (2004) concluded,

So, our investment of billions of dollars over six decades in district, state, national, and international testing for accountability has produced scant evidence that these tests have increased student achievement or provided the motivation to learn. At the same time, we have seen mounting evidence of great harm for some segments of our population. (p. 23)

In contexts in which tests have high stakes — where test scores determine whether or not students can pass from one grade or level to the next, how much funding a school receives, or whether or not superintendents and principals keep their jobs — they take on greater importance than they should, given their nature and purpose. There is also evidence of negative outcomes, such as reduced achievement, increased dropout rates, and reduced graduation rates, especially for minority students (Amrein & Berliner).

As documented by Hargreaves (2003) and many others, testing for accountability, which is central to the larger trend to raise standards through greater standardization of education, has contributed to the de-skilling of teachers as they tailor classroom practices in response to externally generated, tightly structured standardized curricula and assessments.

Hargreaves argues (pp. 79–80) that many teachers have become "casualties" who must

- coach children to memorize standardized learning
- learn to teach as they are told
- undergo in-service training on government priorities
- work harder and learn alone
- treat parents as consumers and complainers
- perform emotional labor
- respond to imposed change with fearful compliance
- trust no one

The last item on the list is particularly troubling, given the evidence cited earlier that trust is one of the key characteristics of schools that are the most successful in enhancing learning for all students.

While greater standardization can demonstrate short-term gains in relatively simple basis skills, it has not transformed schools in the ways that are required so that they better prepare students to live and work in the knowledge society. Such educational reform demands a much *higher* level of professionalism and reflective practice from teachers, the opposite of what has been the outcome of the growing standardization of curriculum and assessment. It demands that schools become places in which all those involved work together to achieve improvements in complex forms of student learning in ways that are responsive to diverse perspectives, experiences, needs, and interests.

Throughout this book I have been arguing that principals can make significant differences through enacting such visions of schooling. So, given the limited usefulness of external, large-scale assessments as tools for school improvement and the potential for harm in their misuse, what can individual principals do to make the best of these forms of measurement? In addition to putting energy and resources into improving classroom assessment, principals can work proactively to enhance the appropriate use of the results of external assessments as part of the school's efforts to improve student learning.

Enhance the School Community's Collective Knowledge

Most parents and members of the community have very little knowledge regarding the nature and purpose of large-scale assessments. The same may be true for many principals and teachers who have long forgotten what they learned about tests and measurement in their teacher preparation programs. Whether we like it or not, external testing has credibility with the public and has real effects on both the work of schools and outcomes for students. While principals do not have to be measurement experts or highly conversant with statistical analysis to become more knowledgeable users of external test results, it is important that they understand the meaning and limitations of those results. With that knowledge, school leaders are better prepared to help their staffs and school communities put the tests in perspective.

- Large-scale assessments are not appropriate tools to use in assessing *for* learning, as discussed earlier in this chapter. Rather, they provide broad, general indicators of student achievement *of* learning. They can document trends and directions, but they have little value in providing information to guide day-to-day instruction, particularly since they are administered too infrequently to provide the ongoing information that teachers and students need in assessing for learning.

- The information provided through large-scale assessments is of most use to determine if systems are making the best use of resources and to monitor trends. For example, broad information gathered from many students might show that students are struggling with problem solving in mathematics or that students are doing well in reading but not so well in writing. Systems might then do further research and determine that there is a need to purchase different instructional resources or to provide more focused professional development for teachers.

- Large-scale assessments sample what students know and are able to do in test situations that do not replicate the everyday contexts in which students learn and apply their skills and knowledge. There have been significant efforts to incorporate tasks that more authentically represent knowledge in use; for example, many large-scale assessments include tasks that require students to actually write instead of responding to multiple choice questions about writing. In a testing situation, however, it is not possible to create the collaborative contexts. the flexibility in topic choice, and advantages of time and writing tools (computers with spell-checkers, dictionaries, thesauri) that a well-structured classroom writing workshop provides. Moreover, the purposes and audience for such writing usually have little or no meaning to the writers.

- There is a difference between standardized, norm-referenced tests and criterion-referenced assessments. The former rank students based on comparisons with the performances of representative groups of students on the test; they also rank schools and districts. They sort students from lowest to highest so that someone is always on the bottom and top, no matter how well the group as a whole achieves. Criterion-referenced assessments compare the individual student's achievement with a standard of acceptable performance, rather than with a norm group. Such assessments are more helpful in identifying learners' strengths and weaknesses in the areas assessed.

In the current context of accountability, principals do themselves, their school communities, and their students a disservice if they remain uninformed about these forms of assessment.

• Reports of test scores on norm-referenced tests translate a student's raw score (the number of items completed correctly) to a grade equivalent. This score does not reflect a student's mastery of a defined grade-level content or set of skills; instead, it reflects the approximate grade level of students in the norm group with that raw score. If a student does very well on a norm-referenced test, it may translate into a grade equivalent much higher than the student's grade placement. It does not mean that the student has mastered the skills and content to that advanced grade level, only that the test makers have extrapolated how students at the higher level would have performed had they taken the test.

• Most of the complex forms of learning that will help students live and work successfully when they leave school cannot be assessed through large-scale assessments. For example, performance on a test cannot tell us how well a student can work with other people, an essential life skill.

Principals should take the time to become knowledgeable about the external assessments administered in their schools. They should know how well the assessments mirror the curriculum and if they are norm- or criterion-referenced. They should find out when and how test results will be reported. With that knowledge, principals can plan how best to help staff and community become better-informed test users. This kind of proactive educational effort will be most effective if the discussions take place prior to test administration and the release of results. As well, incorporating attention to the purpose and nature of external assessments within broader conversations about assessment for and of learning will help put them in context. Then, when assessment results become public, these discussions can be revisited in relation to the specifics of students' performance on a particular assessment.

Provide Positive Support to Teachers and Students

The administration of external assessments can create extreme levels of anxiety for teachers and students, particularly in high-stakes situations. In these circumstances, students are much less likely to perform at their best than when both teachers and students are more relaxed and focused. If the principal, too, is uptight and puts pressure on others, it only exacerbates the difficulties. School leaders can do a great deal to create environments that are supportive, rather than stress-inducing.

• Ensure that teachers and students are familiar with the assessment procedures and tasks.
• Encourage teachers to spend time helping students become comfortable with test-taking situations; for example, if there are time limits, help students learn ways of approaching the tasks that maximize success.
• Review with staff, and ask them to review with students, the purposes for the assessments and how the results will be used. Discuss how the assessments differ from everyday classroom assessments.
• Express confidence that students will do well without exerting undue pressure on them.
• Show that you are on the side of both teachers and students.
• Encourage parents to keep things as positive and stress-free at home as possible. Remind them to keep the assessments in perspective. If schools have engaged parents meaningfully in classroom assessment, they will be

much more likely to cooperate actively in supporting the school's efforts to decrease the pressure on students.

- Make assessment accommodations for students with special needs. The parameters for most current large-scale assessments provide schools with the ability to provide such accommodations. Indeed, in many constituencies schools operate within policy frameworks that require them to make these accommodations.

Described in more detail in Thurlow, Elliott and Ysseldyke, variations can include those related to,

- Setting: such adaptations as small-group or individual administration; use of adaptive furniture or technology; use of a study carrel; or seating close to the teacher.
- Timing: such measures as allowing more time; giving breaks; or dividing administration into several sessions.
- Scheduling: might involve choosing a specific time of day or day of the week; changing the order of subtests; or omitting sections for which accommodations cannot be made (e.g., sections that cannot be translated into Braille or read to a student with a visual impairment).
- Presentation: changes in format, such as large print or highlighting; alterations in procedures, such as using sign language or providing extra explanation; and use of assistive devices, such as tape recorders or computers.
- Response: marking on the test booklet rather than a bubble sheet; allowing use of reference materials; using different response modes, such as pointing or audio recording; allowing student to use assistive devices, such as computers, symbol boards, or Braillers.

- When large-scale assessment results are published, keep them in perspective. Celebrate the positive and use information regarding areas of need to direct future work. Consider the results in relation to other sources of information about student achievement. Continually revisit the purpose of the assessments and remind teachers, students, and parents that the assessments tell only a small part of the story.

Interpret and Communicate Results

Too often, schools are in a reactive mode when large-scale assessment results hit the news. Schools may not even have seen their own results before reporters start calling for interviews. In these situations, principals who are well prepared can provide specific comments about how the school will use the results. Rather than being put on the defensive, such principals demonstrate that they intend to use the information provided by the assessments responsibly. They also can explain where the assessments fit in their overall efforts to enhance student achievement.

Within the school, while keeping a primary focus on improving classroom assessment, principals can engage teachers in discussions of results, focusing around questions such as the following:

- What aspects of learning did this assessment tap into?

Ideally, schools should be the first to know how they have done, so that they have the opportunity to bring thoughtful interpretation to the results. Frequently, it is not possible to pre-empt the publication of results in the newspaper because of the timing and manner of the release.

- What can we learn about students' accomplishment of the aspects of learning assessed through this test?
- How do these results compare with similar assessments administered in previous years?
- How does the information from the assessments compare with what we know about students' achievement as a result of our classroom assessments?
- Were there any surprises in students' performance; for example, did students collectively or individually perform much better or worse than we would have predicted? How can we explain the differences? What other evidence should we collect to gain more insights?
- Based on what we know about our students' achievement in this area of student learning, should we be giving more or less emphasis to aspects of the program? Do we need to rethink how we are using resources? What kinds of professional development might be helpful?
- What kind of feedback should we give students on their performance on this assessment? How can we help them interpret the results in relation to what they already know about their learning?

Having had such discussions as professionals, principals and teachers can then share the results with parents, explaining what they mean for individual students and for the school as a whole. They can describe to parents how the results are being used along with other sources of information to improve classroom and school practices.

Suggestions for Teacher Professional Development

In order to enact the kinds of assessment practices described in this chapter, principals need to focus on teacher professional development related to effective classroom assessment, the use of large-scale assessments, and school self-evaluation. Although all of these are important, the place to begin in setting priorities is with what happens on a day-to-day basis in the classroom.

Each principal needs to plan professional development based upon knowledge of teachers' current practices and with their input. One way of engaging teachers in discussion might be to share the highlights of research that shows the significant impact of bringing students to the centre of assessment. From there, individuals and small groups of teachers might choose one aspect of classroom assessment as a focus; for example, teachers might first enhance their own skills in giving constructive feedback to students and then teach students how to interact in similar ways as they engage in self- and peer assessment. Teachers might document the kinds of evidence they are currently using in classroom assessment and gradually expand their repertoires, involving students in the process.

Building on the insights from their 1998 review of research discussed earlier, Black and Wiliam, along with other colleagues (Black, Harrison, Lee, Marshall, & Wiliam) have been working with a number of secondary schools in England to make changes in classroom assessment. This work is of particular interest because the challenges of changing assessment practices at the secondary level are much more daunting than at the elementary level. Most elementary teachers have more experience in assessing through observation and interaction than do their secondary-level colleagues, who usually work within rotary timetables that

Not only is there strong evidence showing the positive effects of student-involved classroom assessment, but teachers are most interested and likely to be active participants in professional development that is directly related to their teaching.

provide limited time with multiple groups of students. Teaching almost 200 students is a major obstacle to getting to know individuals well and to finding ways to have conversations with them about their learning. Furthermore, secondary schools rely heavily on tests, which primarily serve as assessments of learning.

The professional development initiative led by Black, Wiliam and their colleagues provides possibilities for principals to consider in setting priorities within their own schools. Although the researchers and their teacher collaborators designed the professional development experiences for a secondary context, the four areas in which they focused apply equally well to elementary classrooms. As well, the collaborative approach in which teachers actively engaged in critical reflection on their practices is applicable across all grade levels and types of schools.

1. Questioning

In order to engage learners more fully in learning and to improve the quality of the interactions, teachers worked on extending wait time so that students had more time to think through their responses. They also expanded the range and complexity of the questions posed, so that they could better assess students' understanding of concepts and approaches to problem solving.

2. Feedback through Grading

Research has shown that feedback through oral or written comments has a positive impact on student learning. In contrast, awarding numerical marks or scores has a negative impact, because students focus on their marks rather than on the comments. Teachers worked collaboratively to improve the specificity (giving focus to what is done well, what needs improvement, and how improvements can be made) and quality (drawing students' attention to the key features of what is being learned) of their comments, both written and oral. Students had increased opportunities to respond to comments and to revise assignments based upon teacher feedback. While teachers still had to comply with school policies on grading, they worked around this by assigning marks only after work was revised, keeping marks separate from written feedback, and marking only select assignments.

3. Peer Assessment and Self-Assessment

The teachers found that helping students set goals was one of the most difficult challenges in enhancing student capacities for self-assessment. As discussed earlier in this chapter, students need teacher support in developing a clear understanding of criteria for evaluating any aspect of learning. They need to know what success looks like. Extensive experiences with peer and self-assessment serve as a kind of apprenticeship, through which students develop deeper understandings of quality performance in an area of learning. Peer assessment proved to be a means through which students could learn more about how to give and get feedback. Students were often more willing to accept constructive criticism from peers than from teachers.

4. The Formative Use of Summative Tests

Although the tests focused on assessment of learning, teachers transformed them into contexts for learning by helping students apply more active learning strategies in test preparation; for example, students generated and answered their own questions individually and in small groups. Teachers also gave students opportunities to develop rubrics to guide peer marking of tests, thus giving a clearer focus to the criteria for successful achievement.

See Chapter 2 for a discussion of how job-focused professional development is proving to be a powerful means of improving schools.

The teachers started small, often incorporating one thing that they were confident to try or focusing their change efforts with one class. Working in small groups, teachers tried different approaches and shared their experiences. They developed plans for how to move forward with more extensive implementation. As the teachers engaged in efforts to improve classroom assessment, they realized that they needed to know more about learning theory, about creating supportive classroom environments, and about constructing support and feedback in ways that not only enhance learning but also increase student motivation, confidence, and self-esteem. The focus on improving assessment led to further professional development related to teaching, learning, and other aspects of teachers' practices.

Principals are key to providing a context within which teachers can engage in this kind of ongoing inquiry into their assessment and teaching practices. Black and Wiliam and their colleagues reiterate the importance of principal support. Specifically, they identify the need for principals to

- find ways of providing time for teachers to meet in collaborative groups, and to discuss their work in staff meetings with teachers who are not yet involved.
- review the school's grading policy to reduce constraints on teachers who are working to shift the focus from marks to constructive feedback; for example, teachers might be exempted from a requirement that every assignment receive a mark.
- ensure that the principal or designate takes on leadership for the change initiative.
- work with staff to develop a long-term plan for supporting early initiators, drawing on their expertise in order to extend the initiative to their colleagues, and sustaining changes over time.

As I considered how the insights from this research and teacher development project might help to inform the work of principals, I thought again about Laura's comments cited near the beginning of this chapter. She believed and was acting on the belief that a focus on assessing and communicating student learning was the key to improving student learning in her school. Drawing on her understandings of teaching and learning, and on her practitioner knowledge about working with people and leading change, she arrived at the same conclusion as the research. The relationships among theories and practices are complex and intertwined: theories inform practices and practices inform theories as educators engage in critical reflection. Approaches to accountability that focus on regulating and controlling short circuit this process, limiting growth and development.

In contrast, when those who work in schools are trusted to assume their professional responsibilities to student achievement and supported in their efforts to do so, both adult and student learners are the beneficiaries.

Telling Your Own Story

Through developing a wide range of criteria and collecting many forms of evidence, schools can tell much richer stories about their work than are reflected in test results or external evaluations. Students, parents, and community members can become active participants in composing and revising the evolving story.

When schools seize the initiative by interpreting and communicating the results of external assessments, they engage in a process of what in school improvement parlance is called "telling your own story" (MacBeath; MacBeath & McGlynn). Just as students need to be brought to the centre of classroom assessment to enhance achievement, genuine and lasting school improvement rests upon schools engaging in ongoing self-evaluation. Schools must develop the capacity to set criteria and goals, collect evidence, and communicate what they have learned to multiple publics in order to speak for themselves, instead of allowing those outside the school to speak for them.

As Laura mentioned in the quote cited at the beginning of this chapter, she wanted to find ways to demonstrate why and how students' participation in school assemblies and concerts contributes to the achievement of learning outcomes. Through discussions with staff and parents, the level and quality of such participation could become one of the indicators of student achievement, valued not only because it reflects one of the school's priorities but also because it contributes to meeting external curricular expectations. Laura knew that she needed to make the learning potential of such experiences visible in order to sustain teacher and parent support for their inclusion in the program. As well, students themselves needed to become more aware of how experiences both within and beyond the classroom contributed to their learning.

Schools that are serious about self-evaluation take a learning stance in relation to their performance, engaging in ongoing critical reflection. Principals have key roles to play in creating and sustaining a climate of inquiry in their schools. When principals regularly seek input on their own performances, they not only gather useful information, but also demonstrate what it means to be critically reflective about professional practices.

Thomas Hoerr, a principal in the United States, seeks feedback from staff through a simple survey that he distributes each spring. He asks,

- What should I start?
- What should I stop?
- What should I continue?

Several times a year he invites staff to have breakfast with him and to discuss anything that is on their minds. He also distributes short surveys to parents once a year, in which he asks parents to offer comments on the school's strengths and weaknesses, to discuss how well the school is meeting their individual child's needs, to offer opinions about the school's efforts to communicate, and to provide feedback on whether the principal has been supportive. From time to time, in his weekly letter to parents, he asks them to indicate a single adjective that expresses how things are going.

School self-evaluation initiatives can involve the development of multiple criteria of success (indicators) and the collection of different types of qualitative and quantitative evidence. For example, MacBeath describes a study in which he and colleagues worked with schools over several years. Drawing on the research on school improvement, they identified indicators within ten themes: school climate; relationships; classroom climate; support for learning; support for teaching; time and resources; organization and communication; equity; recognition of achievement; and home-school links. For each indicator, they described the kinds of evidence, both qualitative and quantitative, that schools might use to show how they were doing in relation to the indicator. Further, they listed the types of methods that might be used to gather the evidence: observations, surveys, review of documents, analysis of assessment results, records of attendance and participation, monitoring of discipline incidents, and many others.

MacBeath emphasizes that the framework developed for the study is just an example of what was done in one context. While schools can build on the work of others, most of the learning occurs through the struggle to describe what is important and to determine ways of demonstrating progress towards accomplishing what is important. As those involved in the MacBeath study worked towards consensus on themes and indicators, they debated important questions (p. 150) that generated crucial discussions about values and purposes. Principals might find these questions similarly generative as they work with staff and community in school self-evaluation.

- What are schools for and who are they for?
- What counts as important and what makes for improvement?
- How should success and improvement be measured?

Through giving a focus to such complex and sometimes contentious questions, principals and their schools can become part of larger conversations about meaning and purpose in public education. When schools take responsibility for evaluation processes that enable them to speak for themselves, they can claim a stronger voice in the discussions that have implications for the policies and institutional practices that shape their work. They become active participants in effecting change, rather than simply recipients of externally mandated school-improvement directives.

MacBeath and his colleagues identified these multiple criteria of success, or indicators:

- school climate
- relationships
- classroom climate
- support for learning
- support for teaching
- time and resources
- organization and communication
- equity
- recognition of achievement
- home-school links

CHAPTER 6   Managing to Lead

The dominance of discourses of accountancy or accountability has significantly affected the work of school leadership. Principals are at the nexus of reform, as often fragmented and disconnected change initiatives rain down on schools.

One day during a school visit, as I walked into Laura's office, a bright and comfortable space with artwork and professional books on display, I tripped over a large binder sitting on the floor next to the computer. "Ah ha," I said, "*A Wellness Handbook for the Administrator*. Does it say anything about preventing researchers from breaking their ankles?" Laura laughed and told me that she had received the binder at a principals' meeting the previous day and had dropped it on her way into her office that morning. "I've been so busy, I guess I just didn't notice it there on the floor. Sorry." On the top of Laura's bookshelf were arrayed a series of provincial curriculum documents with colored covers — yellow for math, blue for language arts, green for social studies, purple for health education — and others in photocopied draft versions. District documents lined the next shelf: a policy binder, an operational handbook for principals, and a Human Resources binder. The *Wellness* binder had not yet found it proper spot on the day I visited.

Talking with Laura, I had an image of her leadership work as "bounded by binders." The provincial Department of Education and the district expected her to manage multiple change initiatives in her school at the same time that she orchestrated all the other demands of a small community. That community had nearly 500 adult and child permanent residents, in a constant ebb and flow of in and out of the building and on the end of a phone line. She also had to respond promptly to a perpetually full e-mail inbox that contained urgent messages from administrators in the district bureaucracy demanding that she answer questions, respond to requests for statistical data, and send in reports.

My field notes from January 1999 include the following to-do list that shows just how many tasks Laura was juggling. The principal shared her agenda for the New Year:

1. Work on the school's draft assessment and evaluation policy.
2. Work with the community to form a school advisory council.
3. Revise the school discipline code.

4. Continue implementation of the school improvement plan.
5. Complete teacher evaluations using new board process; support teachers in developing professional portfolios.
6. Carry out student registration under new board policy for Creating School Populations.
7. Acquire more computers for the school; work with staff on using technology to support learning.
8. Plan a retreat for the staff.
9. Gather data on school discipline as part of a pilot research project.
10. Continue with curriculum implementation.

She says, "Some days when I come into my office and contemplate what I have to do I feel like that hour glass that comes on your computer screen when the program is frozen. Where do I start?"

Quote on a piece of paper on the principal's desk:

Being chained to a desk is not all that different from being chained to a stove.

Although Laura and I both laughed at the quote from a calendar for women that one of her colleagues had shared with her, she commented, "There's entirely too much truth to that for me to find it totally humorous."

When I talk to principals about their work lives, I am reminded of the comment I heard at an educational leadership conference several years ago: "Stress is e-mailed down through the system."

From what I have observed and experienced over the years since I spent time in Laura's school, the demands on principals have not diminished. On the contrary, friends who are still principals say that they are tied to their computers. The complaint that the job is dominated by managerial work is almost universal. Moreover, the emphasis on accountability for student achievement has intensified so much that schools are engaged in collecting, analyzing, interpreting, and sharing self-generated data and responding to the results of external assessments.

Sustaining a sense of purpose and enjoyment in the job is definitely a challenge for my friends and colleagues who are school principals. There are ways that principals can negotiate the tensions between those two aspects of administrative work; however, principals themselves are not the total solution to the overload they are experiencing. It's not simply a matter of school leaders learning better time management, as I have heard some senior managers assert. Systems have to decide what kind of administrators they need in order to achieve the improvements in student learning they are demanding. Although the capacity to manage tasks and time efficiently is obviously an asset for a principal, I do not subscribe to the theory that principals need MBAs rather than leadership education. If educational systems want principals to take the lead in improving learning, it seems to me that the people in those roles need to be exemplary educators, not just more efficient managers.

Insights from Research

The International Electronic Journal for Leadership in Learning publishes timely and accessible articles regarding the work of the principal: http:/www.ucalgary.ca/~iejll

As part of my doctoral work, I reviewed a large body of research related to the changing role of the principal. Because of the nature of my own study, I was particularly interested in school-based qualitative research that documented the working lives of school leaders. I was also interested in learning more about how larger social changes, specifically political shifts to the Right across the Western industrialized world, affect public education. While I'm not suggesting that principals need to grapple with the complexities of neoliberal and neoconservative thought, as I did in my studies, I think it can be helpful for practitioners to understand how changes in the external context have been transforming the work of school leadership. Schools and school systems have been part of a reshaping of public institutions in the image of the market. Reform initiatives — such as vouchers, school choice, charter schools, the growth in private school education, and the public ranking of schools based on test scores — are visible examples of the trend to make education a commodity, competitively marketed like any other product.

Creating Schools in the Image of the Market

There are many pressures on principals to emulate the competitive structures and processes of the market. Practices like the ranking of schools through the publication of test results, accountability structures that name schools as failing or successful based on achievement results, and reductions in funding all contribute to an increase in competition among schools. High-stakes testing creates situations in which administrators will go to great lengths to give their schools an advantage, even at the expense of others. In some constituencies, innovations such as vouchers and charter schools pit schools against each other to attract the "best" students and the most socially and financially advantaged parents.

Market mechanisms create winners and losers; they undercut efforts to advance social justice and equity. If I am principal of a school with socially and economically advantaged families in a market system, I give thanks and draw on the abundant human and material resources that I have available to further the advantage of my students and my school. I don't worry very much about the school on the other side of town that serves a high-poverty community. I am likely to be happy to take credit for being the principal of a school with some of the highest test scores and most successful students. Systems in which schools are in competition with each other do not create the conditions within which the best interests of students, especially those with the highest needs, are served. Research (Dempster, Freakley & Parry) with principals in Queensland, Australia, demonstrated that these market values are the source of significant tensions in the work of school leaders, whose personal values reflect a belief in broadly educational purposes of schooling.

Operating schools in the image of the market is fundamentally contradictory to notions of relational leadership. When all aspects of the system are connected through networks of relationships, we assume collective responsibilities towards all the students that we serve. Putting schools in competition with each other works against the development of collaborations across schools that have the potential to benefit all. It also reduces the possibility that principals will create strong professional networks. Such networks provide valuable mentorship to new administrators, give positive support to more experienced leaders, and help all to enhance their knowledge of the contexts in which they work.

Less visible but perhaps more significant have been transformations in the way schools and school systems carry out their work. Making public education more streamlined, efficient, and effective has been a consistent theme. Through restructuring, there have been moves to downsize the educational bureaucracies surrounding schools, vesting more responsibilities at the school level. Accompanying changes in governance in many jurisdictions have created a range of

Schools operate as independent and autonomous entities marketing themselves to their "customers."

A school in which teachers close their doors, horde resources, and compete to do better than their colleagues is a long way from creating the kind of professional learning community discussed earlier in the book.

Across all governance models, schools have taken on much more fiscal and operational responsibility as central offices have disappeared or changed function.

site-based management models in which parent councils take on authority for decisions once made by central offices. At the same time, there has been a growing emphasis on schools demonstrating their effectiveness in relation to student achievement. In governance models that still include district-level structures, the roles of central office staff have become much more focused on accountability and capacity building.

The Principal as Corporate Manager

Within the current context, principals are managers of their sites, responsible for the entire operation and accountable to a variety of publics: students, parents, district staff, the larger community, government, politicians, and the press. Gewirtz and Ball provide a description of the "new managerialism" in public education in the United Kingdom that reflects the international trend to construct school leadership in the image of the corporate manager:

> For the new manager in education, good management involves the smooth and efficient implementation of aims set outside the school, within constraints also set outside the school. It is not the job of the new manager to question or criticise these aims and constraints. The new management discourse in education emphasises the instrumental purposes of schooling — raising standards and performance as measured by examination results, levels of attendance and school-leaver destinations — and is frequently articulated within a lexicon of enterprise, excellence, quality and effectiveness. (pp. 255–56)

As managers, principals are the front-line response to demands for public education to do a better job in preparing students to live and work in the post-industrial world.

Although the discourses of "new managerialism" are increasingly dominant, they are contested by more educative visions of leadership work that more closely reflect the assumptions underlying the discussion of leadership earlier in this book. As Gewirtz and Ball explain, in these conceptions there are, "ideological commitments to equality of opportunity, valuing all children equally, equal and supportive relationships, caringness, child-centredness, comprehensive schooling, assimilation, multiculturalism, anti-racism, girl-friendliness, anti-sexism, developing critical citizens, democratic participation and social transformation" (p. 255).

As the many publics that school systems and schools serve are demanding higher performance from public education, principals working from more educative visions of their work find themselves trying to meet outside expectations but also to be true to themselves.

In a study of one secondary school in London, Gewirtz and Ball documented how a female head, who espoused ideals of collaboration and non-hierarchical management and of schools as sites of social transformation, at times acted in authoritarian ways with her staff. Eventually, she gave up her post for complex reasons; partly because of micro-politics in the school, but also because of the disjuncture between her more educative views and the values and practices of the market-driven policy.

In contrast, her male replacement intentionally worked to make the school successful "as defined by the market/management discourse" and was effective at doing so, demonstrating an ability to be "multilingual" and use different ways to speak about the school when needed. For example, he spoke the languages of public service, the market, financial management, organizational management, and, when needed, the new language of curriculum, having to do with outcomes and student achievement. He had "an ability to argue that market-driven, financial and managerial decisions were compatible and indeed could enhance good educational practice" (p. 265). In the view of the researchers, this was not just a tactic; the head had a genuine commitment to the students and a focus on their welfare.

Relationships among Gender, Leadership, and Management

The study by Gewirtz and Ball raises interesting questions regarding the relationships among gender, leadership, and management. How significant was it that the female leader was unable to reconcile the tensions between what she believed and the external expectations regarding her work, while her male colleague found ways to work within the constraints?

Over the past several decades, as more women have become educational administrators, there has been increased interest in whether and how males and females differ in the ways that they lead. For much of the history of public education this was not an issue because there were so few women in administration. As more women moved into traditionally male roles, beginning in the 1970s and continuing until today, the number of women principals has increased. They are still under-represented in administration relative to their numbers in the teaching profession, particularly at the secondary level and in middle- and senior-administration roles.

As a result of the historic division of labor, with women taking responsibility for the private sphere and men for the public, social constructions of administration until quite recently were associated with the competitive, individual male. Therefore, women were considered unsuited for administration because they were not enough like men.

Theories about leadership have been evolving to incorporate more collaborative ways of working. Over time, women's strengths in relationship building and focus on care, honed in the private sphere, became valued in the public sphere, as well. Australian feminist researcher Blackmore argues that this can be a trap for women leaders, as they attempt to create cultures of care and become the "emotional managers" of school communities stressed by a never-ending stream of change initiatives driven by the marketization of education.

Binary conceptions of generic male (individualistic, competitive, task-focused) and female (communal, collaborative, people-focused) leadership styles are not representative of the diversity among males and females. Real people clearly are much more complicated and varied: many women are competitive and task-focused; many men are wonderful at building relationships. Further, as Blackmore argues, the corporate world has appropriated characteristics seen to be feminine (empathy, strong interpersonal abilities, collaboration) in order to improve efficiency and to increase the competitive edge of organizations in the capitalist economy.

Crafting the administration of schools in the image of corporate management — for example, through promoting entrepreneurial forms of leadership — results in the demands of the market superseding more broadly educational agendas.

With the shift towards new forms of organizational behavior through teaming, collaboration, and shared leadership, the multi-skilled manager (mostly male) now applies generic skills and competencies, drawing on the rhetoric of participation, to achieve outcomes for the corporation. Some feminist researchers, who attribute a greater focus on social justice and equity in schools at least in part to the inclusion of more female leaders, critique the growing influence of corporate managerialism.

Research related to principals and their work paints a much more complicated picture of how both male and female administrators are negotiating tensions

Some feminist researchers argue that the emphasis on competition and efficiency, which they associate with masculinist leadership, is often at the expense of equity and social justice.

between educative and managerial work. Studies of women principals show that their practices reflect many of the strengths associated with female leadership, but that they also are responding to the managerial demands of the job and to the expectations of the external context in creative and inventive ways. Smulyan, who looked closely at the work of three female elementary principals in the United States, found that the principals both changed and were changed by the systems in which they worked. She describes school leadership as "a dynamic process, one in which the principal is limited by the expectations, structures, and social systems within which she operates, but also one in which she is an actor who defines her own role and actions and contributes to a modification of those same systems" (p. 204).

Hall urges feminist leaders and researchers to move beyond rigid feminist approaches that construct masculinist and feminist constructions of leadership as dualistic and that "tie and blind" us.

In discussions of a study of six female heads in England, Hall (1996) showed that all of the women, despite individual histories and differences in current work settings, enacted collaborative forms of leadership. Yet, they also clearly gave overall direction to their schools and responded to the external context. Hall concluded that, "Their accounts and my observations strongly refuted the notion that making the dance floor their own meant dancing like a man" (p. 190). The researcher described how these women, in contexts in which discourses of manageralism predominated, seemed to be evolving a new form of entrepreneurialism that was not primarily managerial. The women worked to make their schools successful in the more competitive environment of local school management, but at the same time attended to educational issues, focusing on the young people in their care. While they rejected the feminist label, they demonstrated their commitment to equity by developing alternatives to competitive and masculinist leadership practices that supported males and females, both staff members and students, equally.

In reflecting upon the implications of the invention of these new forms of entrepreneurship, Hall (2002) acknowledges the dangers, intricacies and complexities of taking such a stance. For example, becoming more entrepreneurial might just mean that these leaders are being co-opted into supporting market forces in education, and thus are not as committed to equity agendas. She argues, however, that there are lessons to be learned from the women in her study — lessons about moving towards "an alternative form of leadership in education that is both ethical and effective" (p. 26). She contends that, building on the insights these women and others like them offer, it is possible to consider how feminist leaders might work towards social justice and also remain in systems that provide "both constraints and opportunities" (p. 26).

Studies such as one Day, Harris, Hadfield, Tolley, and Beresford conducted in England, in which the leadership of both male and female heads was the focus, provide support for Hall's view. The researchers located the study in twelve diverse schools that had the reputation for being effective and had demonstrated their effectiveness with a range of evidence. They asked the heads themselves, as well as teachers, students, ancillaries, parents, and governors, to describe what made the heads effective. Through their analyses, the researchers identified the characteristics of the heads' leadership practices as "values-led contingency leadership" (p. 170). Both male and female leaders were "constantly and consistently managing competing tensions and dilemmas" and they were "above-all people centred" (p. 167). The heads had strong visions for their schools but led with and through others. They were continually reflective about their own practices. Those practices, as they were represented through the researchers' analyses, reflect many of the characteristics often attributed to female ways of leading. While the researchers themselves did not include gender analysis in their study, I think it raises interesting questions about how both women and men are reconstituting what it means to be a female or male leader as they construct their leadership in response to changing contexts.

Principal as Manager and Leader

The research certainly demonstrates that binary constructions of leadership as either male or female, or as either primarily educational or managerialist, smooth over the contradictions and tensions evident in the work of both male and female leaders. As Australian researcher Thomson argues convincingly, "The exhortations of some educational administration researchers (e.g. Fullan 1993, Sergiovanni 1994) to principals to shake off their managerial yoke is arguably unreflexive, if not disingenuous" (p. 14). I agree with Thomson; from my experience, principals cannot possibly work successfully in today's schools without dealing with managerial expectations. Through the concept of "values-led contingency leadership" Day and his colleagues provide a helpful way of thinking about the work of the principal as both managerial and educative. The heads "rarely used their authority to drive through change, or to influence others. Instead, they used their personal rather than positional power to obtain the results they wanted" (p. 169). Within this conception of leadership, "diffuse rather than hierarchical" management and leadership are "mutually reinforcing" and "leadership behaviour is contingent on context and situation" (p. 170).

The dimensions of such leadership, summarized here, offer a number of principles upon which to build leadership practices.

The researchers extend the description through the identification of the following dimensions of the leadership practices that they observed:

- Through direction, actions, and words, the heads helped others in the school community understand their vision and values, and develop a shared focus for their work together.
- The heads provided consistent models for the kind of behavior they believed contributed positively to the achievement of the school goals, and they promoted trust, respect, and belief in the potential of all. They could, however, also be firm in relation to values, expectations, and standards when needed.
- The heads were aware of and managed external environments, engaging in activities with staff to raise their awareness of issues and to involve them in decision making.
- The heads used a range of strategies to engage others as leaders of multiple change initiatives: formal professional development, frequent positive feedback, involvement in decision making, giving professional autonomy, "leading by standing behind, alongside and in front" (p.173).
- The heads, described as critical thinkers, were reflective about their own values, beliefs, and practices, and those of staff members; how their schools were progressing relative to others in local and broader contexts; policies that affected school management, curriculum; and teachers' working conditions.

Implications for Practice

Unlike the "administrivia" that contributes to a sense of overwork and tedium, higher-level activities energize, renew, and make the job of principal worth doing.

The conception of leadership as values-led and contingent on the specifics of diverse contexts provides a way around the question of whether the emphasis should be on managing or leading. As I reflected upon what I learned through my observations and interactions in Laura's school, I could see evidence of those dimensions in her work. Yet, she still struggled with the competing demands of her job, often feeling overwhelmed by the number and range of tasks she juggled throughout the day and often into the evening and weekends. While there are no instant solutions to administrative overload, the suggestions that follow may provide some possibilities for how principals can keep their focus on the higher-level activities described in the dimensions of values-led contingency leadership. Such activities contribute to making the school a positive and productive learning and working environment for both students and adults.

Rethink Management

In the Day et al research, the heads talked about how they viewed leadership and management. Their comments offer a different way to think about management, a way that connects aspects of the principal's role that are often seen as contradictory. One head of an infant school said,

> Leadership and management must coincide; leadership makes sure that the ship gets to the right place; management makes sure that the ship (crew and cargo) is well run. If it's just your vision you will not get to the right place — you must have a combined agreed vision with all the staff on board. You must have a strategy, therefore, for getting agreement. (Day, et al, pp. 38–9).

In a similar vein, the head of a secondary school reflected,

> Leadership is about getting across to the staff where we are now and where we are going. It is not about the mechanisms by which that vision is achieved — that is management. Leadership is also about knowing what to do and being able to raise the morale of staff. (pp. 38–9)

Thoughtful reflection about how to handle school operational issues can become an important part of the intellectual work of school leadership.

Working from the assumption that leadership and management are complexly interrelated within the whole of an administrator's work, I contend that the ways in which educational leaders deal with even the most mundane and routine operational issues send clear messages to others about vision, values, relationships, and purposes. Such decisions affect the teaching and learning in the school. No decision, however small, is neutral. Administrators are involved in such decisions all the time: what teacher should be assigned to which classroom, whether a supply cabinet should be kept locked or unlocked, whether to order desks or tables, whether to spend money on computers or library books, how to deal with graffiti in the washroom. Depending on the choices made, a principal might advance or impede collaborative learning and teaching, enhance cooperation or competition among staff, and build or erode trust.

Thinking about managerial tasks in this way, a principal can transform that aspect of the work into a tool for accomplishing larger purposes. Principals still have to face the externally generated paperwork that seems to be the bane of every principal's existence, but that type of "busy work" is easier to put in perspective if the majority of the operational aspects of the job have more meaning and purpose.

Let Go of the Unimportant

Some of my very experienced principal colleagues say that, if in doubt, they ignore requests in the certainty that if a request is truly important, it will come again.

Even the paperwork burden can be alleviated somewhat with a change in approach. Deciding what is important and what is trivial is one of the key survival strategies for principals. Importance is highly context-specific; what is unimportant to successful leadership in one situation may be a key issue in another. The ability to make these distinctions develops through administrative experience and a good knowledge of a school community. For example, principals learn what kind of parent calls they need to respond to quickly in order to prevent a complaint from escalating into a full-scale crisis, and which ones they can safely let their secretaries handle or defer until a later time. Inexperienced school leaders soon learn that there are negative consequences to the school if they do not attend to requests for information that may affect funding, staffing, resource allocation, or other essentials. On the other hand, principals may choose to ignore or to give less priority to requests that do not so directly affect the school.

Such discernment is also a philosophical issue. When I was an administrator, keeping an open door in order to maximize interactions with people was an essential feature of the way I enacted leadership. For another colleague, responding to e-mail and getting reports done took precedence. While I did not ignore these aspects of the work, I gave them less importance than the "people" part of the job. I tried to keep the paperwork in perspective, doing a good job but not worrying about making things perfect. I decided that I would rather be remembered for the quality of my relationships than for the standards of excellence in my paperwork.

Create a Positive Work Environment for Support Staff

I cannot emphasize enough my strong belief that administrators can have a powerful positive impact on the quality of the work of support staff and on their job satisfaction, through encouragement and belief in their abilities.

Throughout my career I have been fortunate to work with extraordinary people who supported my administrative work as administrative assistants, custodial staff, and paraprofessionals. These individuals brought different strengths and talents to their work, but every one of them contributed in important ways. A principal needs to begin by engaging support staff as fully participating members of the school community so that they, too, share in the school's vision and purpose, and have a role in shaping agendas. In my experience, these staff members then take responsibility for working towards solutions of problems that are within their scope to solve.

When I was an assistant superintendent responsible for a number of schools, many calls came into my office. My assistant, the secretarial and administrative staff, and I shared an understanding regarding the manner in which those calls should be handled. I could trust every one of them to make good decisions about how to respond and about when I needed to become involved. As a result, my time was not tied up in dealing with issues that others could address, and the support staff found that aspect of the work provided challenge, variety, and opportunities to interact with a wide range of people. I know principals who have similar working relationships with support staff, and, as a result, are less tied to the office during the school day.

Move Past Your Need to Control

By relinquishing control, principals enhance their capacities to give direction and focus to the school to a much greater extent than if they attempt to tightly manage all activities.

As a result of my own administrative experiences and through observing many other administrators over the years. I have concluded that moving past one's own need to control is a big positive step towards a happier and more rewarding work life. The most stressed and overworked administrators I know have been those who attempted to control every detail of the school's operation. Such an approach is doomed, because it is impossible to control everything in such a complex context. More significantly, it ties up the principal in attempting to manage the unmanageable, instead of in working at the larger undertaking of developing shared vision, collective values, and productive and trusting working relationships. When all members of the community are working from common sets of assumptions that guide actions and decision making, there is no need for the school leader to attempt to exercise control. In such a context, people other than the principal are more likely to share responsibility for tasks that might otherwise fall to the administrator.

Make Trust and Respect for Others Visible

I have had a few disappointments in people over the years, but, for the most part, when I have trusted and respected individuals and expressed those beliefs through my words and actions, they have exceeded my expectations.

Relinquishing control, especially in a context in which principals are publicly accountable for what happens in their schools, requires a leap of faith based in trust in others. Most teachers want to be positive and contributing members of the school community. All have talents and skills that can enhance the school and benefit students. Some are great organizers who are eager and more than capable of taking responsibility for tasks that keep the school operating smoothly. Others have strengths in curriculum, classroom management, and other aspects of pedagogy that can benefit the entire school. Those that seem reluctant to do their share are often those who have not had their efforts acknowledged or appreciated in the past. Sometimes the demands of individuals' own lives (for example, children or aging relatives) make it impossible for them to contribute beyond what they are required to do in their own classrooms.

In some situations, the principal needs to challenge staff expectations regarding roles. Lambert offers the following suggestions (p. 25) to principals who are working towards the development of shared leadership in their schools:

- When staff members persist in asking permission from the principal, the leader can redirect the question by asking, "What do you recommend?"
- When the staff is unresponsive in a problem-solving situation, waiting for the principal to provide the right answer, the leader might say, "I've thought about this issue in three ways…. Help me analyze and critique these ideas," or "I don't know the answers…. Let's think it through together."

> - When staff members refuse to take on responsibilities that they consider the principal's job, the principal may need to negotiate these roles and responsibilities more explicitly at a staff meeting, discussing the need for everyone to contribute to the community and setting expectations for participation.
> - If principal expectations become a teachers' union issue, the principal should engage all involved in discussion and in working towards a negotiated solution.

Providing support, constructive feedback, and public acknowledgment of accomplishments enhances the possibility that staff members will continue to be active participants in the school. Second guessing, continual checking up, and negative criticism from the principal are likely to discourage even the most positive staff members from getting involved.

Once responsibilities have been delegated, the principal needs to back off and allow those sharing leadership the latitude to work things through in ways that make sense to them. People may not always do things exactly the way the principal would have; the principal has to trust that the tasks will get done and truly believe that there is more than one way to reach a goal or to accomplish an end. In my experience, the solutions others come up with have usually been as satisfactory as my way would have been, and often much better.

Although parents have a different role in school life than staff members, similar principles apply. The principal who is willing to delegate responsibility to parents within agreed-upon parameters can reap innumerable positive benefits. As when working with staff, the principal then needs to express trust in those who have taken on the responsibilities by encouraging them to accomplish the tasks in ways that make sense to them. Again, it is important to have included parents in discussions regarding vision, purpose, and values before vesting them with responsibilities.

Develop Agendas for the School Collaboratively

When staff and parents have had the opportunity to help shape the agenda for the school, they are much more likely to become active participants in enacting that agenda. They will take on responsibility for tasks that they have identified as important. In contrast, when the principal owns the problems and the solutions, the principal ends up doing all the work and/or attempting to coerce others into doing their share.

> Michele Hancock, principal of a high-poverty school in Rochester, New York, describes her efforts to get staff to take more ownership for the school. When she first took on her administrative job, she observed that "entrenched 'I' behaviors had crippled the school" (Hancock & Lamendola, p. 76). Teachers closed the doors of their classrooms and contributed little to the school as a whole. Hancock challenged all professional and support staff and parents to focus collectively on the well-being of students. She distributed a survey to everyone, asking two questions:
>
> - What are the two best things about the school that a new principal should know?
> - What two things do we need to work on or change now?
>
> She, the staff, and the community developed an agenda for action from the responses. The wide involvement of all in identifying the issues of most importance to them resulted in a high level of commitment to the agenda

for change that evolved. Staff members were willing to take leadership and to commit time. Other principals might find these two questions helpful in engaging staff and community, and they might keep Hancock's following reflections in mind as they work through the complexities of such a process:

> Helping people change themselves and their thinking is a difficult task. Many times, I dealt with confused, stressed out, cynical employees who wanted to do better but did not believe in their own potential or in the potential of our students. I learned to really listen to people, acknowledging their feelings without judgment. Gradually, we began to analyze and challenge our beliefs about student learning. (Hancock & Lamendola, p. 77)

Strive for Coherence

The simplest and most effective way for a principal to create coherence in the school is to ensure that all initiatives contribute to enhancing student learning.

In Laura's school, one of the biggest issues was the fragmentation that she and the staff experienced as the result of the number of unrelated initiatives generated externally to the school. Further, they had a number of pressing school-based issues that they needed and wanted to address. For example, there was a school-wide commitment to ongoing efforts to create and sustain a peaceful school, as well as an ardent interest in arts education, enhanced by the efforts of a gifted music teacher and the involvement of community artists. Although all the schools in the district had been engaged in site planning, the implementation of provincial curriculum did not seem to find its way into most of those plans. As well, Laura told me that the arts initiative arose after they had completed the site plan, so they had to work at finding a way to add it to their priorities.

> I recall Laura telling me in an early interview that she was very concerned about being unable to provide the leadership needed in order to implement all the new provincial curricula. She had attended a meeting in which a supervisor had told principals that they should have a three-year plan for implementing the curriculum guides, and she worried about her lack of such a plan. Later, she described how, through reflecting on the ways that she and the staff had been enacting a shared vision for the school, she determined that she actually *did* have a plan for enhancing the program in the school. She told me,
>
>> And I thought, I'm not into that three-year plan thing. But that doesn't mean that there's nothing happening at the school. But you get the mind set that if you don't have a plan on paper that says from September to December we will focus on this, and this is what it'll look like, then it means you don't have a plan. And I don't think that is necessarily true.... So when I left the session, I thought, okay, I need a plan. Well, what I did was go back through professional development sessions that teachers have attended, sessions we've had at the school, conversations that we've had… bank days that teachers have taken and have gone out to different things. And I wrote them all down. And I did it over the past three years, and when I looked at it, I thought, well, there's my plan!

We agreed that it sounded a bit like developing the outline after writing the paper, and confessed that neither of us ever writes from an outline. Instead we jot notes, create webs and lists, write, reread and rethink continuously, developing greater coherence in the writing through ongoing composing, rethinking, and revision.

Creating a coherent plan for a school is very much like writing processes; it is evolutionary and recursive, not linear. The development of formal, three-year plans through improvement planning may provide a structure through which to engage staff and community, but the plans themselves need to be written in pencil. The planning has to be functional, workable, and purposeful in relation to administrators' and teachers' efforts on behalf of the students and the community. Educators have no time to waste in creating plans on paper that cannot be enacted in the complexities of the context within which they work. They need the flexibility to take advantage of unexpected opportunities — such as the invitation Laura's school had to participate in an arts initiative — that advance the school community's shared vision for the school.

The simplest and most effective way for a principal to create coherence in the school is to ensure that all initiatives contribute to enhancing student learning. School leaders are on solid ground when establishing priorities for the school and for the use of administrator and staff time when they can demonstrate connections with student learning. Lots of people have lots of good ideas for projects and activities that involve schools; principals need to learn to say no to those that will divert time and energy from a focus on students. Schools can develop excellent justifications for not participating in initiatives that are peripheral to meeting the learning needs of the students.

Maintain Perspective and a Sense of Humor

In a human enterprise like school leadership, the leader has to expect that the humans, both child and adult, will make life constantly interesting and surprising.

It's easy to say, "Maintain perspective," but much more difficult to accomplish when the papers are piling up on the desk, the e-mail inbox is choked with messages, and everyone seems to want a piece of you. One of the heads interviewed by Day et al offered good advice, "The job has no boundaries so you must impose your own to maintain your sanity" (p. 58). Along with setting boundaries on what it is possible to do and still sustain health and sanity, it's also important to keep in mind that the job by its very nature is unpredictable and complex. The best and happiest principals that I know accept that their best laid plans usually will go awry; they don't beat themselves up if most items on their daily to-do list are still to-do at the end of the day.

Keeping one's head and one's sense of humor when everyone else is losing both is, for me, the sign of a principal who will not only survive, but also thrive on, the challenges of orchestrating complexity. I've never known humor to fail to lighten my load and to help others keep their work in perspective. When I was stressed out over some work-related issue many years ago, my husband gave me a plaque that I have hung in every office I have since occupied. It says,

Blessed are those who can laugh at themselves for they shall never fail to be amused.

On many a day it's been a good reminder not to take myself too seriously.

Conclusion

In the Introduction to this book I posed the question, "Why would anyone want to be a principal?" I hope that the stories, insights, and suggestions I have offered remind practising principals that their work can be intriguing and rewarding, as well as challenging and sometimes exhausting. I hope, too, that the book's message has been positive and encouraging to teachers considering a move into administration. Finally, I hope that readers who fulfill administrative roles outside schools will reflect on how they, too, can give a focus to developing collaborative work cultures across levels of the system.

As I contemplated how best to conclude this book, I was reminded of the difficulties I experienced in writing the conclusion to my doctoral research. Having critiqued conceptions of reform based on "list logic" throughout the thesis, I worked hard not to fall into the trap of summing up my research in terms of the "five key insights" or the "seven implications for practice." Although, in the interests of clarity and organization, I had to give some order to my reflections, I considered them an exploratory collection rather than a list. In closing this book I take a similar stance. I offer some closing thoughts on "big picture" possibilities for practice that have the potential to sustain principals' energy and commitment through giving larger meaning and purpose to their work.

Sustain Hope

Teaching by its very nature is a hopeful undertaking. Most of us chose to be teachers because we wanted to make a difference and we believed in the potential of young people. These days it is all too easy for educators to lose hope and confidence in their capacities to do their best for the diverse range of students who come into our schools each September. Conflicts in all areas of the world bring into schools students who are often traumatized by what they have experienced and need a range of supports to become functioning members of the school community. The creation of inclusive educational settings, too often without sufficient funds to support the vision, stresses principals, teachers, support staff, and parents who want to do more for these most-vulnerable of our learners. Regularly beaten up in the press for their failure to create the "world-class citizens" their many publics demand, schools struggle to accomplish more with fewer resources. What schools attain never seems to be good enough.

Principals have a central role to play in sustaining the hope with which most teachers embark upon their careers. I observe this hopeful stance each year as I work with many idealistic, committed, and gifted people who are learning to be teachers. When they return from their first encounters in their school placements, some of them have pretty discouraging stories to tell about cynical and burned-out teachers who try to give these novices a dose of reality regarding the impossibility of the job. I tell my students to do everything they can to avoid the "walking wounded" who hold forth in too many staff rooms.

Fortunately, however, there are many schools in which principals and teachers demonstrate their unfailing enthusiasm and sense of purpose. Those schools are the places I want student teachers to experience. They are, without exception, schools in which principals provide engaged, positive, and optimistic leadership. They are the places in which there is laughter and celebration of the small and large ways in which students, teachers, parents, and other community members contribute. The principals come in both genders and have different personalities. Some lead quietly and others with more visible panache. They work in different ways, depending upon their personalities and life experiences. Yet they all share a sense of hopefulness about their work and engender the same kind of hopeful perspective within their schools. There is no question that these leaders put students at the centre of everything they do.

The principals sustain hope through connecting with people and ideas. They foster positive relationships within the school and create support systems for themselves among colleagues. They reach out to their communities and invite them to participate in the school. They genuinely want parents to be partners in learning. They see themselves as part of something larger than the school and take the responsibility to participate in those larger contexts. They do their homework in regard to external expectations, forging mutually supportive relationships across the larger system within which they work. They continue to learn through professional reading, conferences, professional development, and graduate study. Through their ongoing learning, they develop the ability to bring critical analysis to experiences, issues, and institutional practices. That analysis helps them work more strategically, employing their social and political acumen. Knowledge and insight contribute to greater confidence and a stronger sense of efficacy.

Bring Values and Ethics to the Centre

When principals bring values and ethics to the centre of their work, they continually reflect upon the beliefs that underlie educational practices, relationships, school culture, and decision making. Begley, writing as Head of the Ontario Institute for Studies in Education/University of Toronto Centre for the Study of Values and Leadership, argues for the use of *values* to refer to beliefs about what is desirable, and reserves *ethics* for culturally bound principles that are called upon in different circumstances. In Begley's view, relying upon culturally exclusive ethics can be troublesome in increasingly diverse educational contexts. He outlines, instead, a multi-level model of *values* — personal, professional, organizational, communal, and societal — that leaders continually negotiate. He argues that schools need "authentic leadership" defined as "effective, ethically sound, and consciously reflective practices in educational administration" (p. 353).

As Begley points out, societies across the world have become more pluralistic. Schools are sites in which diverse, and often contradictory, perspectives meet and often clash. Whether principals are consciously aware of it or not, they constantly deal with ethical dilemmas in their work. Their personal values may differ from what the system expects from them. Their views of the world may contrast with those of their staffs or of individuals and groups within the community. Conflicts that arise in schools are often the result of discordant belief systems. Principals frequently become the arbiters of these conflicts and, as a result, confront ethical dilemmas about how best to move forward. Working through these issues is part of developing shared values and beliefs, as principals lead ongoing dialogue around core issues such as fairness, honesty, integrity, and care.

Australian scholar Brennan describes educational leadership as processes of building stories around issues of ethics with people who work together. This is not defining ethics as universal rules about how to behave; rather it is continual, thoughtful dialogic consideration of the problems that face us in how to live and work together. Baumann refers to this as accepting our moral responsibility. In relation to the current context of public education Brennan argues that,

> Ethical concerns about the purposes of institutions such as education, or about our reasons for working in a profession such as education, about how we should organise our relations with one another, have been evacuated from major government policy, funding and priorities for education. (p. 3)

Many of our structures and practices create distance, as systems continually restructure to become more efficient. Both fear and communication with "a faceless position elsewhere" (p. 3) exacerbate distancing and disconnection. Brennan suggests that administrators move out of the safety and isolation of their offices and devote energy to engaging people in the co-creation of stories that construct shared understandings of ethical practices.

According to Canadian researcher Fullan (2003), the internationally respected author who has written extensively on leadership and school reform over four decades, the heart of public education in a democracy is moral purpose. Education serves a common good; it is the "cornerstone of a civil, prosperous, and democratic society" (p. 3). We expect a great deal from our schools:

> As the main institution for fostering social cohesion in an increasingly diverse society, publicly funded schools must serve all children, not simply those with the loudest or most powerful advocates. This means addressing the cognitive and social needs of all children, with an emphasis on including those who may not have been well served in the past. (p. 3)

There is no doubt that schools are extremely challenged in taking up their moral responsibility. Achieving the kind of social justice and equity that Fullan envisions will require profound institutional changes. Schools and school systems contend with many obstacles, such as current systems of funding and resource allocation, out-dated hierarchical command and control structures, a shortage of people who want to be school leaders, and lack of support and appropriate leadership development for both aspiring and practising administrators. Yet the work of educational leadership, cast as enacting moral purpose, is a means of working towards equitable and socially just public education. As a school principal, in particular, an educational leader can, on a daily basis, take concrete action to effect changes in the current lives and future life prospects of students.

When I talk with principals about what makes the job frustrating, they almost always focus on the workload created through the external demands on their time. This includes being called out to too many meetings, dealing with too much voice-mail and e-mail, having to produce a steady stream of information to feed the bureaucracy, and fulfilling agendas set by those outside the school. In contrast, when they share stories about how they are grappling with puzzling problems within their schools, their conversations show that they are both emotionally and intellectually engaged in meeting the challenges of working in complex and diverse school communities.

Each person has to decide for him- or herself whether the opportunity for such meaningful engagement outweighs the real constraints and workload burdens with which principals must contend. Friends and acquaintances working in other types of jobs in both public- and private-sector settings tell me that principals are not alone in feeling overworked and constantly in demand. Intense workloads are the reality for most people. An advantage principals have, that those in many other professions lack, is the opportunity to do a job that has significant moral purposes. In this book I have provided examples of ways that principals can enact those moral purposes through creating humane, caring, and learning-focused schools, in which both students and adults live and work productively. In a world in which there is much uncertainty, insecurity, and conflict, that kind of school leadership is undoubtedly worth doing. Moreover, it is crucial to all our futures.

Bibliography

Adams, J. & Ferguson, J. (2005) "Teaching students from many nations" *Educational Leadership*, 62 (4), pp. 64–67.

American Association of University Women (2001) *Hostile hallways: Bullying, violence and sexual harassment in school.* Available at http:www.aauw.org/

Amrein, A.L. & Berliner, D.C. (2002) "High-Stakes Testing, Uncertainty and Student Learning" *Education Policy Analysis Archives*, 10(18). Available at http://epaa.asv.edu/epaa/v10n18/

Auerbach, E. (1995) "Which way for family literacy: Intervention or empowerment?" in Morrow, L. (Ed.) *Family literacy: Connections in schools and communities.* Newark, DE: International Reading Association, pp. 11–27.

Barth, R. (1986) "On sheep and goats and school reform" *Phi Delta Kappan*, 68 (4), pp. 293–96.

Baumann, Z. (1993) *Postmodern ethics.* Cambridge, MA: Blackwell.

Begley, P.T. (2001) "In pursuit of authentic school leadership practices" *International Journal of Leadership in Education*, 4 (4), pp. 353–65.

Black, P. & Wiliam, D. (1998) "Inside the black box — raising standards through classroom assessment" *Phi Delta Kappan*, 80 (2), pp. 139–48.

Black, P., Harrison, C. Lee, C. Marshall, B. & Wiliam, D. (2004) "Working inside the black box: Assessment for learning in the classroom" *Educational Leadership*, 86(1), pp. 9–21.

Blackmore, J. (1999) *Troubling women: feminism, leadership and educational change.* Berkshire, UK: Open University Press.

Blair, H. A. & Sanford, K. (2004) "Morphing literacy: Boys shaping their school-based literacy practices" *Language Arts*, 81 (6), pp. 452–60.

Blank, M. J. (2005) "How community schools make a difference" *Educational Leadership*, 61 (8), pp. 62–65.

Brennan, M. (1999) "Off the horses, gentleman, please! New tales and new morals" Education Leadership Online Conference *Educational Leadership for the New Millenium: Leaders with Soul*

Bryk, A.S. & Schneider B. (2002) *Trust in schools: A core resource for improvement.* New York, NY: Russell Sage Foundation.

Chappuis, S. (2004) "Leading assessment for learning" *Insight* (Texas Association of School Administrators), Winter, pp. 18–25.

Chappuis, S., Stiggins, R., Arter, J. & Chappuis, J. (2003) *Assessment for learning: An action guide for school leaders.* Portland, OR: Assessment Training Institute.

Corson, D. (2000) "Emancipatory leadership" *Leadership in Education*, 3(2), pp. 93–120.

Dauber, S.L. & Epstein, J.L. (1993) "Parents' attitudes and practices of involvement in inner-city elementary and middle schools" in Chavkin, M.F. (Ed.) *Families and schools in a pluralistic society.* New York, NY: State University of New York Press, pp. 53–71.

Davies, A. (2000) *Making classroom assessment work.* Merville, BC: Connections Publishing.

Day, C., Harris, A., Hadfield, M., Tolley, H. & Beresford, J. (2000) *Leading schools in times of change.* Berkshire, UK: Open University Press.

Dempster, N., Freakley, M. & Parry, L. (2001) "The ethical climate of public schooling under new public management" *International Journal of Leadership in Education,* 4 (1), pp. 1–12.

Dillon, D. (1984) "Dear readers" *Language Arts* 61 (7), pp. 679–80.

DuFour, R. (2004) "Leading edge" *Journal of Staff Development,* 25(2), pp. 63–64.

Epstein, D., Elwood, J., Hey, V., and Maw, J. (Eds). (1998) *Failing boys? Issues in gender and achievement.* Berkshire, UK: Open University Press.

Epstein, J.L. (2001) *School, family, and community partnerships: Preparing educators and improving schools.* Boulder, CO: Westview Press.

Epstein, J.L., et al. (2002) *School, family, and community partnerships: Your handbook for action* (2nd ed.) Thousand Oaks, CA: Corwin.

Epstein, J.L. & Salinas, K.C. (2005) "Partnering with families and communities" *Educational Leadership,* 61 (8), pp. 12–18.

Fullan, M. (1993) *Change forces: probing the depths of educational reform.* New York, NY: Falmer Press.

Fullan, M. (2003) *The moral imperative of school leadership.* Thousand Oaks, CA: Corwin.

Furman, G.C. (1998) "Postmodernism and community in schools: Unraveling the paradoxes" *Education Administration Quarterly,* 34 (3), pp. 298–329.

Gewirtz, S. & Ball, S. (2000) "From 'welfarism' to 'new managerialism': shifting discourses of school headship in the education market" *Discourse: Studies in the Cultural Politics of Education,* 21 (3), pp. 253–68.

Gurian, M. & Stevens, K. (2004) "With both boys and girls in mind" *Educational Leadership,* 62 (3), pp. 21–26.

Haberman, M. & Post, L. (1998) "Teachers for multicultural schools: The power of selection" *Theory into Practice,* 37 (2), pp. 96–104.

Hall, V. (1996). *Dancing on the ceiling: A study of women managers in education.* London, UK: Paul Chapman Publishing.

Hall, V. (2002) "Reinterpreting entrepreneurship in education: A gender perspective" in Reynolds, C. (Ed.) *Women and school leadership.* Albany, NY: State University of New York, pp. 13–28.

Hancock, M. & Lamendola, B. (2005) "A leadership journey" *Educational Leadership,* 62 (6), pp. 74–78.

Hargreaves, A. (1994) *Changing teachers, changing times: Teachers' work and culture in the postmodern age.* New York, NY: Teachers College Press.

Hargreaves, A. (2003) *Teaching in the knowledge society.* New York, NY: Teachers College Press.

Henderson, A.T. & Mapp, K.L. (2002) *A new wave of evidence: The impact of school, family, and community connections on student achievement.* Austin, TX: Southwest Educational Development Laboratory.

Hoerr, T. (2005) "Perception is reality" *Educational Leadership,* 62 (6), pp. 82–83.

Johnston, P. (1992) *Constructive evaluation of literate activity.* New York, NY: Longman.

Johnston, P. (1997) *Knowing literacy: Constructive literacy assessment.* York, ME: Stenhouse.

Lambert, L. (1995). *Building leadership capacity in schools.* Alexandria, VA: Association for Supervision and Curriculum Development.

Leithwood, K. & Duke, (1999) "A century's quest to understand school leadership" in Murphy J. & Louis, K.S. (Eds). *Handbook of research on educational administration,* 2nd ed. San Francisco, CA: Jossey-Bass, pp. 45–72.

Lingard, B. & Douglas, P. (1999) *Men engaging feminisms.* Berkshire, UK: Open University Press.

Louis, K.S. & Riley K.A. (2000) "Introduction — relational leadership for change" in Riley, K.A. & Louis, K.S. (Eds.) *Leadership for change and school reform.* New York, NY: Routledge, pp. 1–10.

MacBeath, J. (1999) *Schools must speak for themselves.* New York, NY: Routledge.

MacBeath, J. & McGlynn, A. (2002) *Self-evaluation — What's in it for schools?* New York, NY: Routledge.

Manicom, A., Armour, N., Sewell, R. & Parsons, D. (2004) *In the picture...a future with women in trades, science and technology,* Vol. 1. Halifax, NS: WEE Society and Hypatia Association.

Margolis, J. & Fisher, A. (2002) *Unlocking the clubhouse: Women in computing.* Cambridge, MA: MIT Press.

McGinn, A. (2005) "The story of 10 principals whose exercise of social and political acumen contributes to their success" *International Electronic Journal for Leadership in Education,* 9 (5). http://www.ucalgary.ca.~iejll

Myhill, D. & Jones, S. (2004) "Noisy boys and invisible girls?" *Literacy Today,* December, pp. 21–22.

Nemerowicz, G. & Rosi, E. (1997) *Education for leadership and social responsibility.* Bristol, PA: Falmer Press.

Newkirk, T. (2002) *Misreading masculinity — boys, literacy, and popular culture.* Portsmouth, NH: Heinemann.

Nieto, S. (1999) *The light in their eyes: Creating multicultural learning communities.* New York, NY: Teacher's College Press.

Nova Scotia Advisory Council on the Status of Women (2004) *Women's paid and unpaid work.*

Packer, M. (2001) *Changing classes — School reform and the new economy.* Cambridge, UK: Cambridge University Press.

Riley, K.A. & Louis, K.S. (2000) "Preface" in Riley, K.A. & Louis, K.S. (Eds.) *Leadership for change and school reform.* New York, NY: Routledge, pp. xv–xvi.

Riley, K.A, Docking, J. & Rowles, D. (2002) "Caught between local government authorities: Making a difference through their leadership?" in Riley, K.A. & Louis, K.S. (Eds.) *Leadership for change and school reform.* New York, NY: Routledge, pp. 107–28.

Schmoker, M. (2004) "Tipping point: From feckless reform to substantive instructional improvement" *Phi Delta Kappan,* 85 (6), pp. 425–32.

Sergiovanni, T. (1994) *Building community in schools.* San Francisco, CA: Jossey-Bass.

Sheldon, S.B. (2003) "Linking School-family-community partnerships in urban elementary schools to student achievement on state tests" *Urban Review,* 35(2), pp. 149–65.

Smith, M. & Wilhelm, J. (2002) *"Reading don't fix no Chevys"* Portsmouth, NH: Heinemann.

Smulyan, L. (2000) *Balancing acts.* Albany, NY: State University of New York Press.

Starratt, R.J. (2001) "Democratic leadership in late modernity: An oxymoron or ironic possibility?" *International Journal of Leadership in Education,* 4 (4), pp. 333–52.

Stiggins, R. J. (2001) *Student-involved classroom assessment,* 3ʳᵈ ed. Upper Saddle River, NJ: Prentice-Hall.

Stiggins, R.J. (2004) "New assessment beliefs for a new school mission" *Phi Delta Kappan,* 86(1), pp. 22–27.

Thomson, P. (2001) "How principals 'lose face': A disciplinary tale of educational administration and modern management" *Discourse: Studies in the Cultural Politics of Education,* 22 (1), pp. 5–22.

Thurlow, M.L., Elliott, J.L, & Ysseldyke, J.E. (1998) *Testing students with disabilities.* Thousand Oaks, CA: Corwin.

Traves, L. (2000) "Boys catch up and overtake" *Literacy Today,* September. www.literacytrust.org.uk

Weingarten, T. (2005) "When quiet kids get forgotten in class" *Christian Science Monitor,* April 26 (Accessed April 29, 2005 http:www.csmonitor.com/2005/o426/p11s01-legn.htm)

Williams, B. (2004) "Boys may be boys, but do they have to read and write that way?" *Journal of Adolescent and Adult Literacy,* 47 (6).

Further Reading

Chapter 1: Professional Learning Communities

Bascia, N. & Hargreaves, A. (Eds) (2000) *The sharp edge of educational change.* New York, NY: RoutledgeFalmer.

Boreen, J. & Niday, D. with Johnson, M.K. (2003) *Mentoring across boundaries.* Markham, ON: Pembroke.

Boreen, J., Johnson, M.K, Niday, D. & Potts, J. (2002) *Mentoring beginning teachers.* Markham, ON: Pembroke.

Eaker, R., DuFour, R. & DuFour, R. (2002) *Getting Started: Reculturing Schools to Become Professional Learning Communities.* Bloomington, IN: National Educational Services.

Meier, D. (2002) *In Schools We Trust.* Boston, MA: Beacon Press.

Sweeney, D. (2003) *Learning along the way.* Markham, ON: Pembroke.

Chapter 2: Students, Parents, and the Wider Community

Botrie, M. & Wenger, P. (1992) *Teachers and parents together.* Markham, ON: Pembroke.

Davis, C. & Yang, A. (2005) *Parents and teacher working together.* Markham, ON: Pembroke.

Gardner, K. & Chadwick, G. (2003) *Improving schools through community engagement.* Thousand Oaks, CA: Sage Publications.

Girard, S. & Willing, K.R. (1996) *Partnerships for classroom learning.* Markham, ON: Pembroke.

Simmons, J. N. (2001) *School problems.* Markham, ON: Pembroke.

Vopat, J. (1994) *The parent project.* Markham, ON: Pembroke.

Wright, K. & Stegelin, D. (2002) *Building school and community partnerships through parent involvement.* Toronto, ON: Prentice-Hall.

Chapter 3: Schools as Diverse Multicultural Communities

Fay, K. & Whaley, S. (2004) *Becoming one community.* Markham, ON: Pembroke.

Kendall, J. & Khuon, O. (2005) *Making sense.* Markham, ON: Pembroke.

Marshall, P.L. (2002) *Cultural diversity in our schools.* New York, NY: Wadsworth.

Obiakor, F.E. (2001) *It even happens in "good" schools: Responding to cultural diversity in today's classrooms.* Thousand Oaks, CA: Sage Publications.

Parkin, F. & Sidnell, F. (1992) *ESL is everybody's business.* Markham, ON: Pembroke.

Chapter 4: Gender and Schooling

Booth, D. (2002) *Even hockey players read.* Markham, ON: Pembroke.

Cooper, J. & Weaver, K.D. (2003) *Gender and computers: Understanding the digital divide.* Mahwah, NJ: Lawrence Erlbaum.

Flinders, M. (1996) *Just girls: Hidden literacies and life in junior high.* New York, NY: Teachers College Press.

Metropolitan Toronto School Board *Challenging ourselves.* Markham, ON: Pembroke.

Skelton, C. & Francis B. (Eds) (2003) *Boys and girls in the primary classroom.* Philadelphia, PA: Open University Press.

Tatum, A. (2005) *Teaching reading to black adolescent males.* Markham, ON: Pembroke.

Chapter 5: Making Sense of Accountability

DuFour, R., DuFour, R., Eaker, R. & Karhanek, G. (2004) *Whatever it takes—How professional learning communities respond when kids don't learn.* Bloomington, IN: National Educational Service.

Foster, G. (1996) *Student self-assessment.* Markham, ON: Pembroke.

Foster, G. (1998) *Standards for learning.* Markham, ON: Pembroke.

Power, B.M. & Chandler, K. (1998) *Well-chosen words.* Markham, ON: Pembroke.

Sirotnik, K. (2004) *Holding accountability, accountable.* New York, NY: Teachers College Press.

Chapter 6: Managing to Lead

Badaracco, J.L. (2002) *Leading quietly.* Boston, MA: Harvard Business School Press.

Booth, D. & Rowsell, J. (2002) *The literacy principal.* Markham, ON: Pembroke.

McCall, Erin (Ed.) *Principals Online.* www.principalsonline.com

Neilsen, A. R. (Ed). (1999) *Daily meaning—Counternarratives of teachers' work.* Mill Bay, BC: Bendall Books.

Index